WINTER PASSAGE

WINTER PASSAGE

Essays, Memoirs, Journeys

ALAN LITTELL

Six Mile Creek Press, Ithaca

WINTER PASSAGE
Published in 2018 by
SIX MILE CREEK PRESS
902 Giles Street
Ithaca, New York 14850
harrylittell@yahoo.com

Copyright © 2018 by Alan Littell
All rights reserved

Layout by Harry Littell
Copy editing by Nora Littell
Typeset in Adobe Garamond Pro
Printed in the United States of America by Blurb

ISBN: 978-0-692-16624-6

First Edition

The titular article, "Winter Passage," was first published in Parnassus, a Paris literary journal, in the summer of 1960. In the United States, it originally appeared in The New York Times (titled "Freighter Solitaire") on May 27, 1973, and is used by permission. "Encounter in Paris" originally appeared under that title in The New York Times on March 16, 1975, and is used by permission. "Flight" originally appeared in The New York Times (titled "Diary of a Transatlantic Flight") on Oct. 10, 1976, and is used by permission.

Photography credits:
p. 17-Harry Littell, p. 58-Harry Littell,
p. 77-Caroline Littell, p. 98-British Airways,
p. 123-Alan Littell, p. 145-Harry Littell

In memory of
Caroline Littell
1939–2015

CONTENTS

Page	Title	Year
1	Introduction	
7	Winter Passage	1960
16	Final Edition	2013
21	City of Pleasure, City of Pain	2015
30	The Fever Tree on Kimathi Street	2002
36	A Mariner's Log	1998
45	On the Road in a Vanished France	1974
51	Jerdie Harrington Leads a Tour	1988
56	An English Gentleman Instructs	2017
62	The Boy in the Shallows	2016
66	Why Do We Travel?	2017
71	Prodigal Paddy: Writer, Warrior, Rogue	2017
76	Sailing Turkey's Indigo Sea	1991
82	The Man Who Ate Squirrels	2016
86	The Brothers From Wichita	2014
90	Flight	1976
105	Encounter in Paris	1975
111	The Sailor Who Longed for a Hero's Death	2017
116	Whatever Happened to Kernan?	2016
121	Afoot in Europe's High Country	1996
127	Searching for Simba	1990
133	Big Mary's House	1992
138	Twice an Immigrant	2017
145	About the Author	

INTRODUCTION

THE seeds of this book were sown by my elder son, Harry Littell, photographer, teacher of photography, and proprietor of a small publishing establishment based in Ithaca, New York. He had read a newspaper piece I had written that told the story of his mother's strange and perilous journey, as a two-year-old, dodging German U-boats across the Atlantic to England after being evacuated from wartime Egypt, her birthplace. Caroline Littell, née Caroline Jane Penelope Byass, died in 2015, and it is to her memory that this book is dedicated.

My son suggested I put together a selection of articles I had written over many years for magazines and newspapers in this country and overseas. At first, I demurred. I could not identify a unifying theme that connected pieces as diverse as travel, seafaring, politics, memoirs. But in the end, after much discussion, we settled on an idea that brings an apparently disparate grab-bag of commentary into tighter focus. And this is a sense of the passage of time—the evanescence of time. Indeed, for much of what I've written, this notion, this idea of the ephemeral, underlies the tapestry I've woven of people in particular places at distinct times. It is, for me, a special kind of past that in the process of recall sharpens its imagery, becomes magnified: a past in which the force of memory is most intense. The idea of past is the real theme of much of this book.

Many years ago a British writer I've long admired, H.M. Tomlinson, published a book of his essays titled "A Mingled Yarn." In it, Tomlinson created a journalist's vehicle for displaying his meditations on the East End of London, the working-class riverside precinct where he had grown up, and also on the First World War, which he had witnessed as a newspaper correspondent. He collected the pieces in no particular order—the dates ranged from 1914 to 1952. Yet despite the interval separating these occasional articles, there was an underlying coherence to his writing. I would indeed have liked to borrow Tomlinson's title for my own, but that would have been unseemly.

I've titled my book "Winter Passage," the rubric of the first of my essays. The story first appeared in 1960 in a literary magazine published in Paris and was later republished under a different name by The New York Times. Although a narrative of a sea voyage, the titular "Winter Passage" metaphorically suggests, at least for me, the encroachment of age: I am now in my ninth decade. The book's final essay also touches on the sea. This, however, is the tale of the toddler Caroline Byass's 1941 voyage from Egypt to safety in England, and of the grown woman's passage

21 years later in a far grander ship from England to New York, where we would marry. I call the piece "Twice an Immigrant."

Bracketed by these two sea stories, the rest of the volume is, with three exceptions, landbound. The first of the exceptions—it appeared initially in a national yachting magazine, Ocean Navigator—is the piece titled "A Mariner's Log," excerpts from the journal I had kept as a young merchant seaman after World War II. The second, "Sailing Turkey's Indigo Sea," written for newspaper distribution, tells the tale of a 1991 schooner voyage I made in the eastern Aegean, and the third, published in 1976 by The New York Times, takes to the air. In this piece—I have titled it "Flight"—I relate the singular, almost mystical experience of occupying the cockpit observer's seat behind the captain of a British Airways jumbo jet on an overnight flight from New York to London.

The most personal of the book's essays and memoirs are the various pieces recounting the two years, in the early 1960s, when I and my late wife lived and worked in Paris. For both of us, it was a carefree and happy time. But I think the essay I wrote that has affected me the most is the one I call "The Boy in the Shallows." I had an odd affinity with that three-year-old Kurdish child, found dead in 2016 at the edge of a Turkish beach; we shared the same given name, Alan. He had drowned while trying to escape the holocaust that was, and is, Syria. I wrote the piece in a burst of anger. What had happened to him, and to the tens of thousands like him, is an affront to human decency. The boy remains for me a portrait of our peculiar age. I cite his death as a metaphor of brutality, greed, indifference, corruption; and, in case I may have missed something, I invite readers of the essay to fill in the blanks.

The book's gathering of my journalism has been culled from a body of work dating back six decades. In addition to The New York Times, publications I contributed to included broadsheets and tabloids published in most of the country's major cities. I owe a special debt of thanks to the editors of the three Western New York papers in and around the village of Alfred, my home—The Alfred Sun, The Hornell Sunday Spectator and The Olean Times Herald—for offering me the hospitality of their columns to explore, across a span of the past five years, a global range of topics of my choosing. And in concocting this volume of essays and memoirs, I lay bare a journalist's universe of encounters, thought and opinion that readers may find of more than passing interest.

—Alan Littell
Alfred, New York
August 1, 2018

1960

WINTER PASSAGE

JANUARY 1960. I have taken sea passage from New York for Le Havre and board an American freighter whose sides bleed winter rust. I am her sole passenger. My cabin is high above the water, at the after end of the boat deck. It contains two bunks; I select the inboard one. There are three large closets in the pea-green room and an adjoining bath. A framed notice advises me that meals will be served at 7:30 and 11:30 in the morning and at 5 in the afternoon. A Chinese steward fetches my luggage from the head of the gangway. His vocabulary consists of a few mandatory words of English. He and 46 other men and officers make up the ship's company.

At sailing time, I stand on deck; around me looms the vessel's massive bulk, her masts, booms, tangles of wire rigging. I hear the high-pitched dissonance of engine-room machinery. Above the North River wharves, stars shine through rifts in the cloud cover. Sailors clear the littered deck. Men on the bow form a tableau against a naked light bulb. From the bridge,

Winter Passage

which is one deck above where I stand, orders are shouted into the enveloping cold:

"Take in the gangway…."

"Single up fore and aft…."

"Cast off the stern line…."

"All clear in the river, Cap…."

"Slow astern…."

"Midship the helm…."

"Half astern…."

No wind. No ripples on the river. A tugboat brings the vessel's bow around. Men on deck look to the Manhattan shore. The freighter gathers steam and heads south.

The first surge of the open sea. The vessel begins to pitch and roll. Smoke plumes from her stack; the wind carries it astern. She has dropped the pilot, resumed her way, and her course is east. To fetch Le Havre, she must first make landfall at Bishop Rock, a jagged outcrop southwest of England's Cornish coast.

First Day: The endless saucer of the sea. The smell is clean, with nothing of sea wrack in it. Clouds veil the sun. The sea and wind haul out of the east. The wind is brisk and cold. The sea is slatey-looking and flecked with tumbling whitecaps.

The chief mate guides me to the wheelhouse. It stands high above the vessel's flush deck and five cargo holds. The mate points out, in turn, the automatic fire-detection system, the rudder-angle indicator, the automatic steering mechanism, the gyro compass. He activates the radar and discusses its use, speaking

Winter Passage

with authority. He unfolds a chart, on which are inscribed a number of pencil lines. They indicate, he explains, a series of storm tracks moving from west to east.

"We have to worry, not about this," he says, pointing to an area of low barometric pressure off the coast of Wales, "but about this." And his finger describes a circle of low pressure to the west of the ship.

At lunch I take my place opposite the captain in the officer's saloon. The captain is small, ruddy-faced, slack-skinned. He seems a mild-mannered man. He is given to vacant laughter and his eyes move skittishly. He looks fatigued. He pecks at the food before him, which is ample but undistinguished.

Personalities among the crew begin to take form: the chief mate, boyish, imaginative; the third mate, a cynical conversationalist; the second mate, older, a father-figure; the chief engineer, a man of wit; an electrician who is a linguist; an able seaman whose parched face and squinty blue eyes bespeak a lifetime spent at sea—he wears the slouch cap that sailors call a Skid-Row Stetson, and laments the decline of American shipping.

Soon the sun dips below the horizon's rim. The sky in the east is dirty, but with an electric quality that is unsettling. The outside temperature is 32 degrees Fahrenheit and the seas, pushed up by a 25-knot breeze out of the northeast, march on the ship in steep, ordered ranks. At dinner the talk is of ports, ships, ship canals, shipbuilding, and home mortgages. The events of the outside world are unknown; there is no radio news. The men

Winter Passage

and the ship have shaken down into sea routine. A sense of boredom infuses the ship, like fog. The ship is isolated in time and confined to an unscenic world delimited by the constant edge of the sea's horizon.

Clocks advance one hour during the night. This is the first of six time changes. The ship is pitching sharply into head seas.

Second Day: The noon temperature is 34 degrees. The ship has touched the edge of the Gulf Stream. The water temperature reads 60 degrees, or so the engineer on watch reports. Mist forms on the sea. The wind is light in the northeast but the ship rolls deeply to a mounting stormswell. The ship is following an area of high pressure across the sea, but storms lie ahead and also follow.

The ship is independent of all global life. Its routine of watch-on, watch-off, the gray sky, the vast and circular gray sea, these are its only realities. Conversation is repetitious: of ships, their crews, of bookies in Boston, taverns in Amsterdam, whores in Birkenhead, Wilhelmshaven and Hamburg.

And at night, seasounds boom through the lee door of the wheelhouse. In the darkness and without visual references, one's sense of the ship is that she rushes forward with the speed of an express train.

Third Day: In the Gulf Stream. Air temperature 48 degrees. The barometer has dropped below 30 inches and the wind pipes out of the east at gale force eight—about 40 knots, or 45 miles an hour. The ship pitches steeply into 15- and 20-foot seas that

Winter Passage

are patched and scored with grayish foam. The storm system is on the ship's tail; the counter-clockwise flow of air is bringing the thrust of the wind from the east.

Fourth Day: The force of the wind increases. The ship works hard in deep troughs and mountainous crests. She plunges and leaps; she takes green water over the bow; she throws up clouds of spindrift.

Gray sea fuses with gray sky. The vessel rolls 20 degrees to either side. Crewmen lurch comically across the decks or pull themselves along interior handrails. The wardroom mess steward places barriers called fiddle boards around the tables. In the center of each table is a wooden box with condiments and cans of evaporated milk. I eat my soup with the bowl in one hand, leaning with the ship's motion. The rolling and pitching set up a bar to conversation. Meals are an unpleasant business. The incessant effort to balance is irritating and fatiguing.

Late in the afternoon, the chief engineer enters the wheelhouse. He stands quietly behind the captain and stares moodily through the salt-streaked windows to the sea. The wheelhouse is damp and chill; the sea is loud outside. Wind thrums through the wire rigging. The chief engineer speaks:

"Somebody didn't pay."

"You get weather like this if you don't pay your whore," the captain says.

After a time, the wind comes round but without losing strength. At night the rolling is very hard; sleep is difficult. The

Winter Passage

ship creaks and strains. She worries in the sea.

Fifth Day: The sea has moderated. Its surface is rough and confused with a southwesterly stormswell.

The vessel logs 15 knots. The forenoon mate has obtained a sextant altitude of the sun: a measurement of degrees of arc above the horizon. Computations of the observation, the first in three days, place the vessel generally north of her reckoned course. Soon clouds screen the sky and there is no further chance to pinpoint the position by celestial observation.

Sixth Day: The air is warm, the sea rising. The storm center half an ocean to the west of the vessel hardens its outline. Rain falls. The sky is overcast. The barometer drops to below 30 inches and steadies.

By the following day, the wind has built to gale force. It blows out of the southeast. Sky overcast. No sun. The monotony of shipboard life is a stone in one's chest. Fatigue. The mental assault of anecdotes without end about bars and whores from Bilbao to Helsinki.

Eighth Day: A southeast gale blows out of a menacing sky. The seas are high; the ship rolls in a great swinging arc.

By early afternoon, the cloud canopy shreds and the mate on watch, sextant in hand, braces himself on the wet steel deck, feet apart. His body sways like a reed sunk in shifting soil as he swings the instrument's mirrored arm across the calibrated arc, seeking the sun. Soon he finds it. He adjusts the vernier with his right hand, then rushes through the wheelhouse door, holding

Winter Passage

the sextant away from his body. In the chartroom he converts his sun-sight to a pencil line on a chart. The vessel is somewhere on that line. To find the specific point, the navigator will require the stars.

At dusk the sky is the inside of an azure bowl. The line of the horizon is sharp. Stars flash and glitter. The three deck officers calculate rough bearings and altitudes and with preset sextants move about the bridge deck in quest of their targets.

"Did you get the moon?"

"I didn't bother."

"How many stars have you got?"

"I've got two...."

"I've got four...."

"I've got three...."

And in the brightly lighted chartroom, the mates work rapidly with tables and almanacs open before them, computing the ship's position. One after another, the navigators inscribe lines on the chart whose intersection forms a rough asterisk, the vessel's geographic location. Satisfied, the men step back. The second mate's face stretches in a smile. "Well, that's not too bad," he says.

The position by star altitudes places the ship 15 miles west and 30 miles north of where she was thought to have been by deduced reckoning—the calculation based on compass course and speed. The correction made, the vessel moves on across the sea.

Winter Passage

Ninth Day: Bright sky, bright sun. The sea rough, deep blue, ridged with snowy foam. The wind is cold and clean. After a perfunctory fire and lifeboat drill, the second of the passage, the work of landfall begins.

Tenth Day: The vessel makes landfall, Bishop Rock Lighthouse, just on midnight. By morning, in the hard winter sun, the sea is running in 10-foot waves pushed up by a strong northeaster. Foam and spindrift chalk-scar the sea. Clouds cross the sun, patching the sea with shadow, converting bottle-green to blue and purple.

Coastal steamers breast the head-seas. Those going downwind ride easily. Seabirds swoop low in the troughs, suddenly soar toward the sun, their wings dazzling in whiteness.

Now the first daylight sighting of land: boulder-strewn, wave-washed Casquets Island. And behind it looms Alderney. The Channel Islands seem conjoined by a bridge of rocks jutting perilously from the sea.

Salt spray lifts gently over the bow, is caught by the wind, is flung back to dash like gravel against the wheelhouse windows. The air, clear and luminous, appears scrubbed, purged of imperfections. Eyes feast on the varied contours of the land after sea days of horizon rims.

Now after dark. The lightship guarding Le Havre beckons with a bright, flashing light. The moon is high. It silvers the sea. The ship's mainmast, in its path, throws a long shadow across No. 3 hatch. The tops of cradled booms gleam.

Winter Passage

The northeast wind has died. The sea is slight; the ship rides easily. The wheelhouse is dark except for soft points of light from the compass and rudder angle indicator. The engine room telegraph glows red, dimly.

"We're getting a lee now, George," the captain says. "Current turns in our favor soon. Give us a push."

"Looks like it, Cap," responds the second mate. "She smells the barn."

After a time, the pilot climbs aboard. The ship gathers way and moves to the dock.

2013

FINAL EDITION

I WAS saddened to read earlier this year that a venerable name in American journalism, The International Herald Tribune, will be no more. It disappeared from the flag—logo strip at the top of the front page—of that fine English-language broadsheet, published in Paris in one form or another for more than a century, to make way for the marque of its current proprietor, The New York Times.

Fifty years ago, I worked as a news editor for the Paris paper, then identified by a universally recognized rubric, The European Edition of The New York Herald Tribune. We occupied a dingy low-rise on the Rue de Berri, a block from the Champs-Élysées. The editorial office—the so-called city room—was a cramped, austere place of peeling wall paint and of dented desks and tables cluttered with manual typewriters, paste pots, pencil stubs, scrolls of teletype printouts, overflowing ashtrays. Adding to the litter were carafes of wine and the debris of takeout meals from the Berri Bar, next door.

Final Edition

"City room," of course, is a misnomer. We did hardly any local reporting. Wire-service copy eked out by dispatches from the New York edition's reporters and correspondents based in the U.S. and overseas made up the bulk of each day's paper.

In the center of the room, at right angles to the managing editor's desk, a pair of tables had been pushed together to form our news desk. There, three of us scribbled, cut and pasted. We worked in shirtsleeves, ties pulled loose, taking a paragraph or two, say, from the Associated Press newswire followed by a bit more from Agence France-Presse and whatever we could find from United Press to cobble together a pastiche that ran the next morning under the heading "From Cable Dispatches."

Front page of the Paris Herald Tribune, early 1960s. The paper covered the world from a cramped office near the city's main boulevard, the Champs-Élysées.

Winter Passage

We had one added responsibility: editing our two resident columnists, Art Buchwald, a round-faced, cigar-chomping satirist and gadfly, and Robert Sage, a courtly, white-haired author and editor and translator of Stendhal.

Buchwald had turned up in Paris after the war and talked himself into a job at the Trib reviewing movies and reporting on restaurants. He knew no French, which wasn't much of a handicap. One of his editors described him as the "typical bumbling American boy in Paris, an innocent abroad with a sure touch for the irritations and surprises of the average foreign traveler."

Sage was cut from more literary cloth. He belonged to that so-called "lost generation" of writers and artists who had migrated to Paris after the First World War. He was known to have been part of a circle that included Kay Boyle, Gertrude Stein, F. Scott Fitzgerald, Ernest Hemingway. In 1940, as German armies closed in on the city, he and a few other Paris Trib editors managed to publish the paper's one-page final edition before the presses shut down for good until the Liberation.

In my time at the paper, Sage produced travel features and book reviews. Why we of the news desk should have been assigned to read his copy, I do not know. I for one did nothing more than pencil in paragraph markings, for he was a brilliant, elegant, disciplined writer: it would have been a desecration to alter his work. Buchwald, on the other hand, was idiosyncratic. Yet save for lapses in spelling, his copy rarely lent itself to editing and certainly not to rewriting.

Final Edition

Buchwald had a genius for wry understatement and deadpan humor. He composed his columns in a private office. Trailing cigar smoke, he had the sly habit of peering into the city room to see if his offerings had brought forth a laugh or even a smile. I rarely smiled. None of us, I recall, laughed that much. We were too busy moving copy to laugh.

One other writer who wandered into our orbit from time to time was a tall, Swiss-born but thoroughly Americanized descendant of an ancient and noble house of France. Sanche de Gramont was a dashing figure, a Paris-based correspondent for the New York edition. In the States, he had won a Pulitzer Prize for deadline reporting. Later he would reap wider acclaim for his biographies of Somerset Maugham and Franklin Roosevelt, written under the adopted name of Ted Morgan, anagram of de Gramont.

The news desk was flanked on one side by the horseshoe-shaped copy desk, presided over by a slim, middle-aged expatriate with a gleaming bald pate, Roy McMullen. Roy sat in what we called the "slot," dispensing our patchwork of cable dispatches and correspondent reports to his sub editors for final polishing and headline writing.

The financial desk guarded our opposite flank. "Desk" may be laying it on a bit thick. A ratty table presided over by an aging Frenchman made up the financial desk. I knew the financial editor only by his first name, Albert. He had the extraordinary knack of being able to spot transmission errors in the thousands of stock prices cabled daily from New York. Laboring like a clerk in a

Winter Passage

Dickensian bank, he would sort through clouds of paper, knowing intuitively if the share price for, say, AT&T or IBM had been misquoted. Accordingly, he would eliminate the offending item.

For many overseas readers, Albert's operation was the core of our newspaper, and each one of us on the news desk took it in turn to understudy the job. How Albert did what he did was incomprehensible to me. There were no computers; all of that tabular material had to be edited by hand. I, and no doubt my colleagues, frequently uttered a silent prayer to keep Albert from sickness or harm.

My berth at the Trib was a good one without a lot of money in it. But we didn't worry too much about money. Paris in those days was an idyll of youth and promise, and we had a grand time putting out that historic newspaper.

2015

CITY OF PLEASURE, CITY OF PAIN

AFTER an absence of many years, I returned to Paris this October to visit my brother and his wife. Their names are Robert and Victoria. Bob writes novels of espionage. He's lived in France since the 1970s, and, with his wife, who comes from an old French family, owns a turreted medieval pile in the southern part of the country as well as a flat here in the capital. The flat is located in the northern half of the city, on the Rue du Faubourg St.-Martin, at the edge of a 200-year-old waterway known as the Canal St.-Martin.

The flat is too small for guests, so Bob has installed me in a comfortable hotel a 10-minute walk away. I have a bright, airy room overlooking a widened extension of the canal—the Bassin de la Villette—a harbor of sorts filled with pleasure boats and restaurant barges.

It is a lovely area. People jog or stroll. Some play pétanque, a game of bowls. I see around me the old and the young: men and women ambling arm-in-arm; small children on scooters;

Winter Passage

lovers clasped in embrace. I see Arab women in headscarves, and African exotics in flowing peacock robes.

The adjoining streets are a festive precinct of cafés, their sidewalk terraces shaded by awnings of brilliant yellow, red or green. One, with its seductive invitation to "boire, rire et manger"—drink, laugh and eat—inscribed on an overhang of canvas, sums up the spirit of the district.

But I don't wish to romanticize. In the Paris of 2015, the sidewalks of my brother's neighborhood are befouled by dogs. Pizza boxes, plastic wrappers, wine bottles and beer cans litter the streets. And strollers smoke incessantly, particularly children in their early teens.

For the smokers, the governing ethos is that tomorrow is a mirage; one lives for the pleasures of now. But perhaps the city has always been thus. It surely was in my day; and that was ages ago.

*

Today my brother and I take the Paris Métro from the Place de Stalingrad station to the Vavin stop, on the other side of the city. We will visit the old artists' and writers' outpost, Montparnasse, where my wife, Caroline, and I had set up housekeeping, such as it was, in a small hotel in the early 1960s.

Montparnasse is now an enclave of tourists seeking a raffish, bohemian Paris that no longer exists. But it is pleasant, still, to wander these streets and to amble past the terraces of the storied grand cafés—the Coupole, the Dôme, the Select,

City of Pleasure, City of Pain

the Rotonde—that face one another in friendly, or not-so-friendly, competition across the broad expanse of Boulevard Montparnasse.

From the boulevard, Bob and I walk up Rue Vavin. It is a street of shops and cafés that extends in the direction of Rue Notre Dame des Champs, where Ernest Hemingway once had lived, above a sawmill, at No. 113. We cross Boulevard Raspail and continue on Vavin for a few steps until we reach No. 21, the Hotel Danemark.

Seeing the place again brings me back to the time when my wife and I had worked in the city. The Hotel Danemark was in effect our first real home together, and we were happy here. Our room, I recall, had an oversized bed, a chair, an armoire, a sink (a luxury then), a naked light bulb hanging from the ceiling—nothing more. But it was cheap and clean. The hotel had five floors. They were linked by a narrow spiral staircase. A toilet cubicle about the size of a telephone booth was recessed into each landing. The proprietor and his wife occupied a ground-floor apartment, where, for a few extra francs, we could use the bath.

The proprietor's name was Roger Nurit. I remember him as a robust young man with a thin, handsome face. For those of us struggling to learn the language, he spoke French slowly with a clear, precise accent. His wife was a jolly woman called Jannine. They had two small children, a girl, Arlette, and a son, Jean.

Winter Passage

It is Jean now who presides behind the front desk. He is a slim, fit-looking man of middle age. A few feet to his right, an elevator has replaced the spiral staircase, and the rooms, I learn, have been equipped with telephones, TVs and modern baths. Like the updated amenities, the daily room rate has also been brought into the 21st century, climbing from the dollar and a half we once had paid in old French francs to about $140, the U.S. equivalent of European euros.

I ask Jean for news of his family. We converse in French. His sister and mother are well, he says. His father has died. I tell Jean I am sorry to hear it. I speak of my wife. I tell him that she, too, is dead. He murmurs words of sympathy. My brother and I go on our way.

*

A day or two before I am scheduled to fly home, I accompany my brother and his wife to an evening salon for artists and intellectuals given by friends of my brother's, a wealthy couple living on the Rue de Grenelle. The street slices through the heart of one of the city's oldest and most historic quarters. The couple live in a late 17th-century townhouse a short walk from some of the landmarks that Paris is famous for: the Eiffel Tower; the military parade ground known as the Champ de Mars; and the Church of the Dome, a masterpiece of French classical art and architecture and the site of Napoleon's tomb.

We are greeted by our hosts in a room aglow with paintings of the Renaissance. Books and journals spill from tables and

City of Pleasure, City of Pain

shelves. A sculpted frieze decorates the cornice of a 20-foot ceiling. Our fellow guests, architects from California, are here to study the monuments of Paris. A white-jacketed butler circulates silently, bearing a tray of champagne.

The room's centerpiece is the Steinway that at one time belonged to the French avant-garde composer Erik Satie. An American pianist living in Paris has been engaged to play it for us. He performs pieces by Debussy and Ravel. And as the pianist's fingers glide over the keys, he turns toward his audience to explain how French orchestral modernism morphed a century ago into the American ragtime compositions of Scott Joplin and the show tunes of George Gershwin.

The party breaks up at midnight, and a taxi carries us back across the city to my brother's flat. We chat for a few minutes on the sidewalk in front of his door and I take my leave. I walk along the deserted quays of the Bassin de la Villette to my hotel.

* * *

In 2016, I arrive in Paris for my second visit in as many years. I barely have had time to unpack before my brother escorts me on a tour of streets and boulevards that I recall as enclaves of vitality and urban pleasures, but now are dotted with an overlay of squalor and listless misery.

For one thing, the district—the city's so-called 10th borough, or *Arrondissement*—has yet to erase memories of the horror of 2015, the November terrorist attacks in which scores

Winter Passage

of residents were gunned down. Many died on the terraces of cafés just off the Canal St.-Martin. For another, the migrant crisis of France had spilled over from the encampments of the coastal city of Calais to a hellish landscape of beehive tents in the shadow of the elevated Stalingrad Métro station, about a block from my brother's flat.

And so my brother leads me on an excursion through the forlorn destitution of thousands of mostly Sudanese and Eritrean men living rough under the Métro's overhead girders. As we walk, weary faces peer at us from tent flaps. We can see mattresses and bedding brought out to air, plastic containers of rotting food, overflows of trash, and ranks of portable toilets set up by the city authorities.

But there is, and remains, another face of Paris. On most days during my stay, my brother and I take our lunch in one of the old traditional cafés of the quarter, an establishment of smoke-stained wooden walls, antique cast-iron radiators. The food is without reproach. My brother invariably orders a huge pot of tiny mussels. He pronounces them superb. For my part, and mindful of the afflictions of foreign travel, I am less adventurous.

While Bob feasts on his beloved mussels, I delight, for example, in a plate of savory herrings in oil with onions and boiled potatoes—one of the great dishes of provincial France—or in a garlicky salad of *crevettes*, or baby shrimp. Our meals are accompanied by fresh, crusty baguettes and excellent French

City of Pleasure, City of Pain

beer on tap. As is customary, the bill includes tip. We leave a few extra coins on the table to signify appreciation.

*

Now evening. My brother, my brother's wife and I walk along Quai de Valmy, on the west side of the canal. The street lamps have come on and from the Quai de Jemmapes opposite, their reflected light glitters on the still surface of the canal. The water is black as pitch. There is a brooding quality to the scene. The murderous attacks of 2015 are not forgotten. A few blocks away, on the far side of the canal, streets had been turned into an abattoir, a killing ground, and I am ill at ease.

As the three of us walk on this warm fall night, we can see ahead of us the terraces of cafés spilling onto the sidewalk. The terraces are crowded. I have a sense that the drinkers are wary. Perhaps I read too much into this. Yet like all of Paris, they are surely mindful of last year's carnage. Cigarettes aglow, glasses in hand, they glance up to watch us as we brush past.

We dine at one of the showplaces of this part of the city, the Hôtel du Nord. It is situated on the Quai de Jemmapes at a point where the canal bends sharply southeast. It is a lovely restaurant: walls of pastel blue, red plush banquettes, gleaming silver, starched napery. We order deep bowls of a Vietnamese specialty that is all the rage in Paris, *bo bun*. We are not disappointed. The steaming stew of rice noodles, greens and minced-pork spring rolls is spicy and delicious. A full-bodied sauvignon blanc, a white wine from Sancerre, south of Paris,

Winter Passage

complements this superlative meal.

*

The Musée d'Orsay is, for me, the most beautiful of the city's adornments. A cavernous former railway station in the heart of central Paris, it is filled with a matchless collection of 19th-century French impressionist painting: masterpieces of color and light by Renoir, Monet, Manet, Pisarro, Degas. My brother and I work our way through the galleries, then break for lunch in the museum's vast dining hall.

Seated at a nearby table are two couples got up in the opulent garb of Victorian Paris. The women wear flounced floor-length satins and crinoline; the men, morning coats and capes. Only a mile or two from the squalor and despair of the refugee encampments, the museum is hosting a costume ball of revelers in period dress.

*

The street on which my brother lives is a block from the canal. The district is virtually indistinguishable from any other of the city's middle- and working-class neighborhoods. I note a laundromat, a grocery store, a bakery, a florist's, an Indian takeout, a sandwich shop, a scattering of cafés.

Still, there are two curiosities. On my daily walk, I pass the Salon de Thé Arabesque, an Arabian tea house. Here, swarthy men smoke hookahs and play backgammon at small, round sidewalk tables. A step or two down the street, hidden behind the plate-glass window of an unmarked storefront, is a syna-

City of Pleasure, City of Pain

gogue. Nowhere to be seen is the Star of David or a plaque lettered in Hebrew. Jews do not advertise themselves in Paris.

Yet make no mistake; the place is a synagogue. A pair of heavily armed soldiers in battle dress stand guard outside. They nod pleasantly to me as I walk by, and return my greeting when I say *bonjour*.

2002

THE FEVER TREE ON KIMATHI STREET

IN the center of Nairobi stands a tree with a smooth yellow bark and a canopy of fernlike leaves. Botanists call the tree *Acacia xanthophloea*. Yet because it grows for the most part where malaria-bearing mosquitos breed, ordinary people throughout Kenya and the rest of East Africa matter-of-factly refer to it as a fever tree.

What makes the existence in Nairobi of *Acacia xanthophloea* so unusual is that this particular variety of African thorn likes plenty of water and fresh air. Nairobi for the most part has enough water. But the air is corrosive with exhaust fumes. A day's journey south, however, in Tanzania's Ngorongoro Crater, a 10-mile earthen bowl filled with zebra, lion and elephant, I have seen forests of fever trees. The air here is clean and sweet. When the afternoon sun touches the crater's rim, the trees glow a deep chrome yellow, as if lit by an inner fire.

Ngorongoro is a place where elephant rub their hides against the trunks of fever trees, stripping the bark. And I have seen

The Fever Tree on Kimathi Street

these lovely trees along streams edged with papyrus in the vast savanna known as the Serengeti, the upland plain of short- and long grasses rolling hundreds of miles from northern Tanzania into southern Kenya.

Far up the dusty track that serves as the main road west through the Serengeti, past the granite outcrops called Simba Kopjes, I have seen the carcass of an impala fawn draped like a tattered rug across the limb of a fever tree, where a leopard had dragged it safe from scavengers.

Once, in the scorched yellow-gray veldt of the central Serengeti, I watched a young lioness rise from the shade of a fever tree watered by a nearby stream. A few yards upwind, a Thomson's gazelle trotted down to the stream to drink.

Fine boned and tawny coated, tail twitching like a metronome, the Tommie is the most appealing creature of the African wilds. But the lioness had small appreciation for aesthetics. She was a player in a very old drama, one that was neither farce nor tragedy, and that had no moral. The lioness, stalking, furrowed the tall grass. Suddenly she lunged, then sauntered back to the tree with the bloodied gazelle grasped in her jaws.

Unlike fever trees elsewhere in East Africa, the one I remember so well in Kenya's particulate-laden, high-rise capital was hemmed in by metal and glass. It occupied an open-air courtyard, in front of the Stanley Hotel, on Kimathi Street. The courtyard served as a sidewalk café, as it still does, but a second-generation acacia, smaller than the original, now grows on the site.

Winter Passage

The Thorn Tree Café is a popular rendezvous, as widely known in Nairobi as the Café de la Paix is in Paris. I liked to come here on a hot afternoon and sit at one of the tables in the shade of a green-and-white metal umbrella, with the larger shade of the old fever tree—it climbed about nine stories, almost level with the hotel roof—dappling the tile floor.

Sipping a glass of Tusker beer, I enjoyed looking out through the shimmering haze to a thoroughfare of rushing cars and open-windowed buses. Ramshackle pickup trucks swayed alarmingly under the weight of standing passengers. Across the street, women draped in bright khanga wraparounds wandered into or out of the Uchumi Supermarket.

But I especially liked watching the young campers just in from the bush. Their getup and appearance were redolent of adventure. They were streaked with sweat. They wore dirt-stained shorts and scarred boots. The equatorial sun had reddened their knees. They traveled in pairs, conversing in English, German, Dutch or French.

Many of them, I knew, had hitchhiked, or had driven their own Land Rovers, from the southeast, from the great Kenyan game reserve at Tsavo. They would have come up the hot tarmac from Voi and Mtito Andei along the plateau that skirts the Nyiri Desert.

Others had journeyed from the gritty and gullied terrain of Amboseli, several hundred square miles of volcanic ash that lies at the foot of Mount Kilimanjaro. They would have risen at dawn—

The Fever Tree on Kimathi Street

when the mountain's frozen cap gleams with a pale, rosy light unobscured by cloud—and taken the straight road from Namanga, on the Tanzanian border, through Kajiado and the Kapiti Plains. Maasai pastoralists, hair smeared with fat and ochre, prod cattle along this road.

Some of the campers had rambled in from the Mara, in the west, an extension of the Serengeti; and a few had come from Kikuyu country in the north, where green hills planted in coffee surge to the crags of Mount Kenya.

Turning into the café, the campers invariably strode to the tree. Mounted on a square frame around its bole were bulletin boards holding scraps of notepaper under a latticework of elastic tape. Occasionally the campers would pluck a message from the rack. Then they either hurried off, or, if the communication lacked urgency, slipped their packs, fell into a chair and beseeched the waiter for a brace of cold Tuskers.

For so long as old Nairobi hands can remember, the fever tree in front of the Stanley Hotel has doubled as a poste restante, a place where mail is held until called for or forwarded. Before Kenya had a reliable mail service, a letter to an upcountry white farmer, say, in Thika or Gilgil, would have been pinned to the tree. A traveler headed in that direction would have carried the missive—perhaps weeks or months later—to its destination.

Nowadays, Kenya's postal system works just fine. Letters mailed in Nairobi can reasonably be expected to reach Gilgil or Thika, or even more distant Malindi or Mombasa, on the Indian

Winter Passage

Ocean, in two or three days. The sort of notes still found on the fever tree are to and from travelers of no fixed domicile.

Most of the messages are in English, the lingua franca of this part of the world. Unsealed, they are there for anyone to read, and have become a minor tourist attraction in their own right. Some of them are elegies to youth and freedom, hinting at loss:

"Interested to see if this odd address is genuine. Life is quiet. Time collapsing in on itself, but it's free and people are helpful. See you next term."

Some sound a note of bravado. They suggest an easy familiarity with the African continent and with its exotic place names. Implicit in their texts is nostalgia for an irrecoverable past—for a white man's Africa; for Africa as playground:

"We're going up to Lodwar for the weekend, then to the Mara, then to the coast…."

"Looking for a lift to Isiolo, Wadir or Mandera…."

"Leaving Nairobi tomorrow for Arusha; unfortunately can't wait any longer as there's a chance Sean may be able to catch a flight to Lusaka…."

"I'm at the Igbal Hotel but heading north in a day or two to see the Samburu, then back to Nairobi in a week…."

"Can we meet at the Driftwood Club in Malindi….?"

"Looking for riders to Uganda willing to climb the Rwenzoris…."

Some messages disquiet. In the banality of their phrasing, in their lack of embellishment, they have the quality of a fail-

The Fever Tree on Kimathi Street

ing voice. They play on our emotions like the brittle strands of memory; we seem to have heard, or read, them before. Signifying illness or death, they seek a son or a daughter adrift on the empty plains of East Africa:

"Please call dad."

In the old days, runners would have been dispatched to the cardinal points of the compass with copies of the appeal held aloft in cleft sticks. Now there are no runners. For messages such as these, the only possibility of succor is the fever tree on Kimathi Street.

1998

A MARINER'S LOG

I SAILED sporadically from 1949 to the second half of 1956 as ordinary seaman, able seaman and quartermaster in freighters and passenger ships running between New York and European ports. Excerpts from the journal I kept during my voyages offer vignettes of life in the U.S. merchant marine in the years soon after World War II.

*

JANUARY 26, 1949. Victory ship *Lt. James E. Robinson*, with general military cargo for Bremerhaven, from New York. —Staten Island; rain and sleet all day. Battened hatches 2 through 5. My fingers bled at the nails from hauling canvas tarpaulins over the hatch boards. The stuff was stiff as iron. Rain soaked through my clothes; I was wet to the skin. Knocked off and went below. Fo'c's'le (cabin) amidships; pea-green bulkheads and a pair of double berths, the room clean and warm. I had dinner aboard: curried eggs and rice—then a drink ashore just outside the pier sheds. I shot a few games of eight-ball. Back to the ship and turned in.

JANUARY 27, 1949. Foredeck was coated with slush. We hoisted tarps on No. 1, working barehanded to grip the canvas. There was no other way. We swore at the canvas, smashed it down with our fists, manhandled the strongbacks in place over the top. The bosun (deck foreman) felt around the hospital tucks for loose flaps. Chips (ship's carpenter) hammered in wedges between battens and coaming cleats. At the winch controls, one of the deck gang dropped the booms into their cradles. The rest of us stripped preventers, wing guys and schooner guys and got the gear stowed. There was one more job, and the bosun sent me up the foremast to do it. The ladder was slick with sleet. I climbed as carefully as I could, without gloves, clenching spun-yarn lashings in my teeth. At the crosstree I edged out onto the foot rail, holding on with one hand. With the other, I threaded the yarn through the schooner block and made it fast. There was no safety harness, and my hands were numb with cold, but I managed to inch back to the ladder and get down.

Towboats ranged alongside, a white frosting on their decks and fittings. A crane picked up the gangway and swung it ashore. Dusk now. We cast off the lines and backed into the channel. The tugs pushed us around, then we steamed downstream past Fort Wadsworth's green flasher. We slowed, dropped the pilot into his launch off Ambrose. Later, south of Montauk, still on soundings, we beat into a building sea. Staggered is a better word—the wind was gale force, out of the northeast.

Winter Passage

JANUARY 28, 1949. Sick as a dog but standing lookout watch, 4 to 8, on the bridge. At dawn the ship pitched like a hobby-horse into the troughs. The sky was full of exploding wind and streamers of clouds. Winter in the North Atlantic.

FEBRUARY 12, 1949. Bremerhaven. The café was on a street that had not been knocked flat in the war. It had paneled walls and a frosted-glass door. Cigarette smoke rose to the beams. The proprietor shook hands with patrons as they came in from the street and the patrons went from table to table shaking hands with one another. They drank dark beer. A blind man played a melodeon. Some of the patrons got up to dance, stamping their feet until their faces turned red and shone with sweat.

FEBRUARY 13, 1949. I came down on the train from Bremerhaven. A frozen country, hard and rutted. Men and women in loden walked along the tracks. Wood smoke blew from cottage chimneys. Three and a half years after the war, this was a place out of time, innocent of memory. Then we came to Bremen. The train slowed for a bend and I could see the city. It was black with sooty snow, broken buildings. Walking into town, I made my way through piles of brick. The streets stank like fishing boats after the catch has been hoisted ashore.

*

OCTOBER 3, 1949. Former troop carrier *Gen. J.H. McRae*, with war refugees for New York, from Bremerhaven. —In the open sea west of the Scilly Isles; wind northwest, Force 7. Heavy weather. Waves slamming against starboard side. I relieved the

A Mariner's Log

quartermaster for his coffee break. I struggled to keep the course. I was steering a snake. The ship's head fell off 15 degrees to either side. From the wheel, I went to bridge lookout for the rest of the watch, 12 to 4, on the starboard wing—the bow was shipping green water. I peered over the dodger (protective parapet) but could see nothing for the scud. I began to doze. Suddenly we took a monster on the beam; my feet flew out from under me and I started down a ski-slope to the open pipe-rail and probably into the sea. But the third mate—he had been standing at my side—somehow got a hand on my collar and held fast until the ship rolled level. I dragged myself upright, pressed my face against the dodger. I said nothing. The mate said nothing. There was nothing to say.

At sea in the Francis X. McGraw, *one of the many merchant ships the author sailed in after World War II.*

Winter Passage

*

JUNE 3, 1950. Victory ship *Frances X. McGraw*, with general military cargo for Bremerhaven. —Eight days out of New York. Steaming east, English Channel. No wind. Flat sea. Haze. My wheel at 0520. Compass rasping in its bowl as I gave and took spokes. At 0640 I moved to the bow. Hills of Wight visible on the port bow, but indistinct in the mist. Couldn't see the Needles or St. Catherine's Point. Passed two vessels close aboard: close enough to make out their names. One a Belgian boat. The other a squat Liberty ship, a Prudential tub. We were soon in fog. Our horn began to blast. In the intervals, I thought I heard dogs barking. We stood miles off the land but the imagination ran riot. Later: Fog lifted. The pilot came aboard at Dover breakwater. We steamed into the North Sea. Goodwin Sands and Galloper behind us. The wind picked up and started to drive the sea a bit.

JUNE 4, 1950. We fetched the Weser at sunup. Light breeze and easy swells on port side—NNE or thereabouts. Cloudless sky. Ahead was a flat country: wide bends in the river, stands of trees, greenswards, red-roofed gabled houses, church steeples. A painter's landscape.

Towboats alongside, and the smell of mud, oil, hemp, rotting fish. We got into the lock, waiting for the water to rise. Five girls stood on the cobbles calling out, asking for this man or that. An obscenity shouted. The girls laughed. And then mooring lines to the windlass, stopping off and making fast. There was an undercurrent of excitement throughout the ship. Suits were brushed, shoes polished. The promise of a night ashore.

*

MAY 11, 1956. Passenger/cargo liner *Geiger,* with passengers and military cargo for Bremerhaven, from New York. —Sponged grease from davits, messed about in the lifeboats checking water cans, first-aid kits, the rest of the gear. The world drenched in sun and wind. Hot meal waiting below. The good life. Still, there was dissatisfaction, a sense of dislocation. Conrad's line: "The beginning an illusion, the disenchantment more swift." Life at sea. What was the point of it? Something to do with rectitude, or virtue—a virtuous life. Or was that the illusion? But enough. Thinking still of going up for my mate's ticket once I've put in my time. Off watch I plowed through Bowditch and Dutton (navigation texts), and a book I got from the third: "Stability and Trim for the Ship's Officer." Righting moment, metacentric height. A crash course in physics, heavy going.

MAY 16, 1956. A damp raw day. Landfall at Bishop Rock. Ship rolling her side down in NW swell. Foul-weather work, serving ladder rungs with tarred marlin. My hands were stiff and sore. A mechanical job: pass the spool, pull it round. The bosun's mate wandered by: "Boring, hey?" Yes, boring.

MAY 19, 1956. Painted davits, spliced and dog-eared a nine-inch mooring line. I finished on the bow as the North Sea began living up to its miserable reputation. The wind blew cold and hard, raising whitecaps.

Winter Passage

MAY 23, 1956. Westbound leg, coming up to Southampton docks. Went aloft with the bosun to the truck of the main, as high as you can go on this ship. We rigged a U.S. flag to trip open at a pull on a line leading back to the deck, 100 feet below. We sat astride a small yard at the truck as one would straddle a fence post and grinned down at a gaping audience.

MAY 24, 1956. Cleared the land; sea and wind NW, near gale force. The vessel pitched hard all day, and the passengers were sick. Wind soon got up to whole gale, NW, and the vessel rode badly, pounding down to her bottom plates. We rode up one side of a wall of water and skidded down the other. Unpleasant business.

MAY 25, 1956. Weather moderated. By evening we were rolling easily with a short steep sea abeam—northerly.

MAY 30, 1956. Fetched Nantucket Lightship. The *Geiger* had a bone in her teeth—she could smell the barn. And so ended another trip: 21 days, two ports, some 7,500 nautical miles.

*

JUNE 15, 1956. Second voyage of the *Geiger*, with passengers and military cargo for Mediterranean ports, from New York. — Tied up in Leghorn, parting one bow line in the process. The mate insisted on our taking too many turns on the capstan. The line, under strain, couldn't surge or slack. It parted like a cannon shot.

Hot, and a murderous sun. Went ashore for a beer on the quay. A mistake. I came back aboard with a headache and lay

A Mariner's Log

down for a rest, but fell asleep. We were to sail at 1800. I awoke to a moving ship; rushed forward to find an angry bosun wrestling lines with a couple of ordinaries. I lent a hand stowing gear. At dinner, one of the ABs had a gash over his left eye and blood on his shirt. Another missed the ship. The trip had barely begun.

JUNE 18, 1956. Tied up in 100 degree heat in Tripoli, no tugs. But plenty of wind. Had to take enormous leads with bow and stern lines, then work the ship to the inside of a breakwater jetty before getting out the springs and breasts. Again we lost a line. Ashore, cloistered houses, lattice work and filigree, high stone walls with bougainvillea tumbling over them. Horse-drawn cabs were on the streets, and a smell of manure in the hot and by-now windless air.

JUNE 21, 1956. Through Piraeus breakwater in a stiff breeze and chop. Tied up in a dust storm and parted two more lines—the whip end of one nearly smashing my ankles. This is a bloody dangerous trade.

JUNE 23, 1956. Istanbul. Tied up at the Maritime Terminal. This is a city I have liked in the past. Wandered about the covered bazaar, then came out on the old tent makers' street; followed the lanes downhill from the Suleyman mosque to the spice markets at Eminonu. On the other side of the Galata Bridge, I could see one of the Black Sea steamers for Trabzon casting off. The *Geiger* lay a hawser's length behind, starboard side to a floating landing stage.

Winter Passage

JULY 4, 1956. Westbound from Gibraltar. Rain and fog. The ship's horn trumpeted all day, putting us on edge.

The bosun asked me to go bosun's mate next trip. I thought about it. But I told him no. I've had enough. I've decided to leave the sea.

1974

ON THE ROAD IN A VANISHED FRANCE

HOVERCRAFT to Boulogne: a cushion of downblasting air keeps us aloft a few feet above the narrow straits. Dover breakwater—our starting point on England's southeast coast—receding in curtains of spray. Then a soft landing on the sands of Boulogne. Smiles from the customs agent and gift packets of Gitane cigarettes. "Welcome to France," the agent says.

The smell of fish and sea wrack in the air, and soon out of town on Route Nationale 1. With my wife, Caroline, and our two sons, I drive south across the region called Artois and Picardy: shuttered houses behind high stone walls, the road running straight between flanking poplars through midsummer fields of corn and wheat. We roll past Mobil, Shell and Total stations.

"Do they speak American here?" my younger son says. "Some people do," I say. Satisfied, he lapses back into sleep.

I have borrowed for the excursion my English mother-in-law's Volkswagen minibus, a transport of indeterminate age. The vehicle sways like a ship. Through Abbeville, Poix and Grandvil-

Winter Passage

liers. The signs pointing east to Amiens, Doullens and Albert, the chalk ridges of La Boiselle and Pozieres. The great killing ground of the Somme, in 1916. Fifty corpses a year still dug up from the chalk by the ploughman's blade. Trees edging distant crossroads swim up on the horizon like images in a mirage. We are showing France to our sleeping sons. We are showing France again to ourselves.

Slab-sided blocks of flats rise in a landscape; soon we are in the northern outskirts of Paris. We roll through the ancient city gates at Porte de la Chapelle. Cobblestones, cafés and exhaust fumes. The light beige of Notre Dame and the Louvre. The monuments of Paris scrubbed clean as honey-colored stone. I battle through traffic to the Boulevard Raspail, in the heart of Montparnasse. Rodin's Balzac shelters in a leafy bower. The vista a mélange of ubiquitous cafés, the sidewalks thronged with strollers, and with *clochards* snoring over their wine-soaked bundles in doorways and alleys.

"Well, what do you think of it?" I say. My elder son, who is ten, remains silent. What indeed does he think?

On the Rue Vavin, my wife and I are remembered by the proprietor of an old hotel of the quarter, and our rooms are inexpensive and plain. Now after dark. The nearby Café du Dôme, a literary landmark of the 1920s, is all a-glitter with mirrored light. We stop on the terrace for coffee and soft drinks. My younger son is lost in a comic, the older boy plainly bored.

*

On the Road in a Vanished France

The day is fair and Paris wears a quiet, unhurried face. We cross the Seine by taxi to the Champs-Elysées and one of its tributaries, the Rue de Berri. Here, at the newspaper where I worked in the early 1960s, nothing has changed. A litter of yesterday's debris: papers, pencils, paste pots. The dusty scent of nostalgia. We stroll later along the boulevards of Montparnasse under a soft pink sky. The Montparnasse Station has disappeared. Falstaff's—a drinking place we once knew—that, too, is gone, and my wife and I are strangers in a city that for a time had been our home.

*

Our day starts badly. Cold drizzle. Leaving the parking garage, I drive bumper to bumper in misty rain. Soon, at the south side of the city, traffic eases. We are on the Autoroute du Sud, a four-lane toll road that reaches some 600 miles past Lyon to Avignon, Aix and Nice. My wife sits next to me with a road map in her lap. The boys snooze on settees behind us.

Now in sunlight, we climb through a range of hills and descend to a plain past Beaune and Macon. Near Lyon, we leave the autoroute. We skirt the city in the direction of Grenoble and the southeast. A few miles along, I guide the bus through an old coaching gate to the sheltered courtyard of a country hotel. There are vacancies. My wife and I order coffee and cognac in the bar, the boys milk and cake. A television set is trundled in, tuned to a variety show, and the boys are pleased. An American touchstone.

*

Winter Passage

Our route next morning takes us southeast. Soon Alpine masses rise in rocky escarpments and soaring peaks. We move up the steep road into the mountains of Dauphiné, the sun bright, the gray of the north giving way to the faded pink and beige of the south. Medieval villages bathed in strong light, shutters blue and green, café terraces shaded from the sun by awnings of orange and red.

At the confluence of the Buëch and Durance, our road rises and falls in hairpin bends and dizzying ledges hanging from outcrops of upthrusting rock. We pass Digne and Castellane, the outboard wheels of the bus within feet of sheer drops. The steering wheel is slick with sweat. My wife consumes Gitanes. The boys stare at the immensity of sky and rock.

The road becomes easier. We descend through fields of wild lavender into Grasse. The streets are perfumed with the scent of pine and eucalyptus. And beyond the steeply terraced hills of the town, we can see the blue wash of the Bay of Cannes. We coast down to Mouans-Sartoux and from there find our way to the village of Castellaras, a few miles distant.

*

My brother, Robert, who is a novelist, lives in this private domain of some 80 houses perched high on a hill. Cannes and the sea are five miles to the south; in the northeast, snow-topped Alpine ranges. The village is a cluster of mock-Provençal farmhouses with thick insulating walls and windows set back in deep recesses. There is a sense here of lassitude. Sun. The intensity

On the Road in a Vanished France

of color. The existence of an outside world is denied by this mountain fastness.

The next day we wander along the coast road on a sightseeing expedition to Mougins, the ancient commune where Picasso once lived, and from there to Cannes. The city is harsh and frenetic. Cars jostle one another for space. A plethora of shops and cafés. The sun is strong. There is little shade. Along the Croisette and beaches, Americans with backpacks stretch washed jeans to dry on jetty rocks.

At dusk, the quays of the Old Port are thronged with strollers. Boats rock in the dark water. We treat the children and their two French-speaking cousins to pizza and Cokes. We are on the second floor of a crowded restaurant. The air is warm. An accordionist makes his way among the tables, and my younger son deposits a coin in the musician's money pouch.

*

We set off from Castellaras on our return journey across France. We drive on the autoroute westward to Aix. We speed across a desiccated brick-red earth. Red hills and scrub pine. Muted colors shading into one another—a landscape by Cézanne.

Far to the north, we take the main road through Bourbonnais to Moulins and Nevers. By way of Prémery and Clamecy, the road winds through the country's heartland on a high plateau planted in wheat. Past Fontainebleau, we drive on the ring road around Paris in the direction of Arras. We drive through Abbev-

Winter Passage

ille to Route Nationale 1 and reach the coast at Boulogne. We have traveled close on 2,000 miles in ten days.

We arrive too late at the Boulogne docks—we have missed the afternoon hovercraft flight. Our tickets are transferable to the Dover car ferry, which leaves shortly from a nearby quay. But we must be quick; it's the last crossing of the day. We queue for the ship and soon drive aboard.

My wife and I break into smiles of relief as the vessel slips through the breakwater, points her bow north along the chalk cliffs to Cape Gris Nez. There she veers off into the green choppy seas for England.

1988

JERDIE HARRINGTON LEADS A TOUR

"IS it the historical society outing you're after?" the man said.

"It is."

"Then you're in the right spot, for sure," he said. "But don't get mixed up, now, with that other lot, the Pioneers. They'll be meeting here for their Sunday walk."

"Pioneers?"

"You've never heard of them, now? They've gone off drink. Taken the pledge."

It was my introduction to the cordiality and sly banter of the Irish of Bearhaven, where strangers are received as honored guests but where a man who declines to raise a glass of whiskey or stout is viewed with mild dismay.

I had come looking for a bit of Ireland off the tourist track. What I found—an arthritic finger of rock and moor jutting into the Atlantic in the country's far southwest—did not disappoint.

The Beara Peninsula is a forgotten 30-mile sliver of the county of Cork. Bearhaven loosely designates the deepwater harbor

Winter Passage

and town of Castletownbere. Both lie midway along the peninsula's south coast between the head of Bantry Bay, at Glengarriff, and a gale-swept promontory known as Garnish Point.

Castletownbere provides a convenient hub for exploring the scenic riches of the surrounding countryside. The old fishing port is an austere but agreeable place, with a long main thoroughfare of shops and row houses and busy pubs.

A small hotel, Craigie's, and several bed-and-breakfast establishments cater to the few travelers who meander this way.

*

Gerald Harrington—"Jerdie" to all who know him—is the jovial, red-faced chairman of the Bearhaven Historical Society. Sunday after mass in Sacred Heart Church, he marshaled a 10-car field convoy of visitors, teachers, farmers, fishermen.

Once out of the square, we headed west along narrow coast roads. The air was gray with mist and drizzle. Ten miles from town—past Dunboy Castle, ancient seat of the region's O'Sullivan overlords—we pulled to the side and followed Jerdie on foot across a boggy field.

A mound of slab stones held our attention: the grave of an Irish chief. A thousand years old; possibly older. No one knew for certain.

"They measured the remains," someone said, "and it's a fact he was nine feet long, a giant of a man." The Irish have a passion for the arcana of their past, which shades from myth to fact and occasionally back to myth again.

Jerdie Harrington Leads a Tour

From the burial site we drove north under the brow of the Slieve Miskish Mountains. The mist had begun to lift. Now we turned into the hills and climbed through a high pass. An immense panorama opened before us—a vista of moor and plain and the distant island they call Skellig Michael, thrusting from the sea like a jagged tooth.

Close by, shafts of sunlight played on the brilliant green of walled sheep pastures and tiny white cottages plumed with peat smoke. We coasted down to a color-washed village, Allihies, to amble among the fenced-in pits of abandoned copper mines.

In the village burial ground, we read the gravestone epitaphs of long-dead Hanleys, O'Sullivans, Harringtons and Sheas. On a tussocky knoll stood the crumbling ruin of a stone chapel. Connie Murphy, a school teacher from Castletownbere, told us it was called Kilnamanagh: destroyed in the 16th century, he said, at the time of the Protestant Reformation.

*

There is no set itinerary for a visit to Beara. The peninsula's attractions are as varied as the paisley pattern of its tattered shoreline. The wise traveler wanders at will.

The road running north from Castletownbere cleaves a remote, empty country. The tumbledown cottages that litter the moors are century-old legacies of famine and flight. At Eyeries, the road curves east past tiny fishing harbors guarded by eroded rock. Beyond Ardgroom and Kilmakilloge Bay, it tunnels through the luxuriant forest of Derreen, fragrant with the scent of moss and dripping ferns.

At Lauragh, the road shrinks to a track as it doubles back across the peninsula's spine, rising south into barren hills greened by a scattering of fertile fields. The terrain is wild and melancholy. To left and right soar the crags of Knockowen, Coomacleghane, Lackabane. Cataracts plunge from the heights.

Below, a horseshoe valley drops to a lakeside plateau speckled with sheep. The road scales the 1,100-foot saddle of Healy Pass, then turns down in corkscrew bends through a waste of bog and rock to Bantry Bay.

*

Night in Castletownbere. At Craigie's Hotel, on a spit overlooking the fish piers, the dining room tables had been pushed to the walls. An accordionist tapped out hornpipes and country airs.

Couples—for the most part women in their sixties and seventies dressed in a finery of tartan and tweed and pleated silk—grasped one another about the waist, revolving with easy grace across the floor.

A few blocks away, at Twomey's pub, Mrs. Lil Twomey—a grand, friendly women—presided behind the plain wooden bar. As patrons arrived in ones and twos, a stranger was introduced.

Pints of creamy-headed stout stood ready at hand, drawn from the tap. One's health was proposed; one proposed back. Mrs. Twomey commented that it had been a poor season for the fishing, "what with the weather and all—three fine weeks in

Jerdie Harrington Leads a Tour

June, and that was it."

As so often happens in Ireland, the talk turned to friends and relatives across the sea. "Not a family on Beara that doesn't have someone in the States or in Australia," said a sheep farmer from Ballydonegan. "Nothing here for them. No jobs."

Jerdie Harrington appealed for the name of the Massachusetts shoe-manufacturing town near Boston where many of the Irish had settled. "For the life of me, I can't remember it," he said.

His pint untouched, Jerdie went out into the street. In a minute or two, he returned.

"It's come to him now," a man said, "away from the smell of drink."

Jerdie raised his glass in salute.

"Brockton!"

2017

AN ENGLISH GENTLEMAN INSTRUCTS

UNCLE Bruce taught me something about wine. "Uncle," though, may be a bit of a stretch. He was my wife's uncle, an English wine merchant—exemplar of a vocation that not a few of his country's glitterati to this day scorn as "being in trade."

Yet bottling and selling wine is not like hawking soap or cigarettes. It was, and remains, a gentleman's profession. And make no mistake: Bruce Todd was a gentleman. Whether in casual tweeds or workaday pinstripes, he was, always, impeccably dressed and groomed. His silvery hair swept back neatly from a broad forehead; a mustache, also white, and horn-rimmed glasses lent to the ensemble an air of decorative solemnity.

One of my two brothers-in-law addressed him simply as "Uncle," dropping the Bruce. His sister, my mother-in-law, Constance Mary, called him "Bru." He called her "Con." His dozens of godchildren—he never married—and people like me, who had married into the family, called him "Uncle Bruce." I would not have dared to say "Bruce." He welcomed a certain level of fa-

An English Gentleman Instructs

miliarity from outsiders, yet still kept people not of his blood at arm's length, as one would surely expect of an English gentleman. Familiar, yes, but not too familiar.

When first I met him, in the early 1960s, Uncle Bruce served as chairman of a firm of some half a hundred wine-and-spirits shops scattered throughout southern England. The head office lay, of course, in London. The firm's name was Findlater Mackie Todd & Co.

Uncle Bruce imported wine mostly from France and sold it under the house label. He also sold sherry, from Jerez, in Spain; port, from Portugal; and a respectable Scotch whiskey, which he called Jock Scott. Uncle Bruce himself, true to his trade, was a fairly heavy drinker. Yet even for someone of his superb constitution and build—he was a compactly constructed six-foot-two—his intake was prodigious. He consumed each day up to three or four bottles of wine, sherry and vintage port, apparently to no ill effect.

From childhood, Bruce Todd had been an ardent Catholic. He was passionately committed to the works of his Church. He made, for example, frequent pilgrimages to the shrine of Our Lady of Lourdes, in southwestern France, where miraculous healings have been claimed. At Lourdes, he pushed wheelchairs and helped carry litters laden with the dying.

His home was a sprawling country house, Maryland, on the outskirts of London. The property was contiguous with the grounds of St. Mary's Convent School, which my wife, Caroline, had attended as a small child during the war. Uncle Bruce was

Winter Passage

renowned for the occasional sherry parties he would give for the school's teaching sisters.

Uncle Bruce visited the village where my wife and I lived, in the far west of New York State, several times in the 1970's and '80's. Voluble and outgoing, he became an unmistakable presence in shops and restaurants, and also at one of the district's Roman Catholic churches, where he regularly attended Mass.

In addition to his churchgoing, I vividly recall taking him to autumn football games at a local university. Like the soldier (and war prisoner) he once had been, he—though a British national—would snap to attention at the playing of the national anthem. He would stand ramrod straight, thumbs extended from clenched fists and pressed smartly against trouser seams.

Bruce Todd, English wine merchant of the old school, in a characteristic pose.

An English Gentleman Instructs

Because he was in wine, we made obligatory tours of the vineyards and wineries bordering the shores of New York's Finger Lakes, an hour's drive from my home. Despite his own expertise in viticulture and winemaking, Uncle Bruce would listen with rapt attention to the talks given by our guides.

At the tasting bars, he would sample whatever was on offer—the great, the good, the not-so-good—with always an exclamation of pleasure. He never uttered even the slightest criticism of a particular wine. For this British guest in a foreign country, any carping would have been seen, at least in his own eyes, as "bad form."

But I digress. My own education in wine began in London at a luncheon Uncle Bruce gave in the boardroom of Findlater House, his company's headquarters. The date was May 30, 1963. The guests, all except myself knowledgeable about wine, had been invited not simply to sip and spit out, as was the custom among professionals when sampling their products, but to drink, discuss and debate some of the outstanding vintages of the day.

I have the menu pasted into a scrapbook. We began with a 1953 Forster Jesuitengarten, a tawny, sweetish Riesling from a small German vineyard that had been making wine for 500 years. (A glance today at Google will tell you that collectors now bid up the Forster at close to $4,000 a bottle.) Next we pushed on to two of the splendid fruity reds of the Bordeaux region of western France, a Château Cantemerle 1950 and a Château Margaux 1934.

Winter Passage

We closed with a Château d'Yquem 1945, a rich, sweet, golden-in-color dessert wine said by one distinguished commentator to be the "undisputed monarch" of Bordeaux's Sauternes—a heavy but heavenly elixir to be drunk slowly, and brooded over.

Around me, there was spirited conversation. I had nothing to contribute. As an American unschooled in wine, I was out of my element. But my companions at table that noon had no such inhibitions.

With a deft twist of the wrist, they twirled their glasses. Prompted by Uncle Bruce, they commented on the rivulets that flowed from rim to stem. They argued about "bouquet," or aroma. They debated the virtues and possible flaws of taste and aftertaste.

I drank steadily. I knew that what I was drinking, especially those reds of Bordeaux, were glorious wines. But at that first exposure to the fabulous, the historic and the merely celebrated, I could not have told you why they were supreme. Wine education required study. Wine drinking—field work—took stamina and practice. It was heady stuff, literally and figuratively. And so I got through the wines and the luncheon of gulls' eggs, and moved on, more or less intact, to two-for-the-road thimblefuls of Findlater's port and brandy, which capped the session.

Bruce Edward Todd died in his 90th year, in March 1997. His Requiem Mass was offered at the Cathedral Church of Our Lady & St. Philip Howard, in Arundel, on England's south coast. In an affectionate tribute inserted into the program, my wife's eldest brother noted that Uncle Bruce, son of a wine merchant, had been

An English Gentleman Instructs

educated at Trinity College, Cambridge, "where in the secure knowledge that a place awaited him in the family business, he kept a dog, went to the cinema every afternoon, and made friends.

"Starting work in London…he led an active social life and drove, very fast, an open Bentley and a Railton straight-eight….

"Bruce's most notable characteristics were his unfailing cheerfulness and kindness, which led to widespread popularity."

The requiem reading accompanying the Mass was both a mystic philosophical essay and a profound leap of the imagination, written a century ago by a canon of the Church, Henry Scott Holland. It contained little of Catholic dogma. Instead, the shade of someone recently dead—perhaps the spirit of Uncle Bruce himself—consoles the living:

"Death is nothing at all; I have only slipped away into the next room. I am I and you are you. Whatever we were to each other, we are still. Call me by my old familiar name, speak to me in the easy way which you always used….

"Why should I be out of mind because I am out of sight? I am but waiting for you, for an interval, somewhere very near, just around the corner…."

And the reading ends:

"All is well."

2016

THE BOY IN THE SHALLOWS

I'VE pinned a photo to the wall behind my desk. It reminds me of a couple of things, and I'll tell you about them.

A small boy—he looks perhaps three years old—lies face down in the shallows at the edge of a Turkish beach. He is not paddling. He's dead. He wears a red shirt and blue shorts. The papers say he drowned somewhere out in the Aegean Sea and washed ashore. He and his family were part of that exodus of Syrians escaping, or trying to escape, from the holocaust of their country. His mother and brother died with him.

These are the facts of his life. There are no other facts. He did not live long enough to have facts.

I have a singular attachment to the boy in the shallows. We share the same given name. Alan. It must mean something in Syrian Arabic, or in the boy's Kurdish dialect, though I have no idea what that might be. The name probably doesn't even sound the way we say it, in two syllables clear and crisp.

Alan is common enough in the U.S., and in England, too,

The Boy in the Shallows

and, for all I know, in Syria as well. And so I have this connection. The boy in the shallows is also, at least for me, a portrait of our age. The image says something about brutality, greed, fear, ignorance, indifference, corruption, grief. Readers can fill in the blanks. There is plenty of room on the page.

What I think is this: we in our country have ships. We have the crews to sail these ships. I think we should have sent a ship. We might have saved that boy and others like him.

So there's this business of the name. At the same time, I am reminded of something else. In the years after the Second World War, we—I mean the United States—collected people like Alan and his family from camps all over Europe. They had a label. We called them "displaced persons." We'd swept them up from the rubble of a dozen countries. We also salvaged those few surviving remnants of the concentration camps, Jews, gypsies, and so on.

I've read that between 1948 and 1952, we transported to America more than 400,000 of Europe's destitute. We carried them in a fleet of aging and battered ships that once had hauled troops across the globe.

I worked in one of those ships. I was 19. I sailed as a deckhand, an ordinary seaman. Let me tell you about the first of the two voyages I made, in the fall of 1949, on the transatlantic refugee run. The story is instructive. Getting close to people seeking haven is my other connection to the boy in the shallows.

My ship had departed New York bound east for the north

Winter Passage

German port of Bremerhaven, then Europe's main emigrant assembly point. We docked at that city's mile-long steamer quay and almost immediately began loading fuel and stores for a fast turnaround and the trip back to the States. It was a bright, warm morning in mid-September. I remember standing at the rail as a passenger train moved slowly along the pier and clanked to a stop a few yards from the foot of our gangway.

I think I saw about 1,000 people clamber out of that train. There were children of all ages. There were men and women, old and young. The adults clasped the youngest children tightly to them. All these people had big white name tags fixed to their lapels or looped round their necks. They wore a motley assortment of clothes and carried rucksacks or cardboard suitcases. Some only had parcels done up in string.

Once on board, the women, girls and smallest children were herded forward and several decks down to the old troop dormitories, fitted with pipe berths stacked in tiers. The men and boys went aft.

We sailed within hours. Our course lay west. The ship rode easily enough, but at the end of the second day, in the open Atlantic south and west of the English coast, her motion became more pronounced. A storm was making up in the west and a swell had risen out of the sea.

All that night and the next day, a westerly wind chalk-scarred the sea. The wind hardened, rising to gale force. Laboring under reduced speed, the ship staggered into cresting waves. She

The Boy in the Shallows

rolled, lurched and slid. Spray, carried by the wind, struck in sheets.

The passenger compartments had become impossibly foul. A couple of the ship's officers went below to spread ammonia, driving the people up and out. On deck, we rigged lifelines. Soon, the refugees lay gray-faced on cold steel with wind and spray sweeping over them. Yet the very young children pranced and tumbled, riding with glee the monster's heaving back.

The westbound passage took a week and a half. But not until we had fetched the lee of New York's harbor approaches did the wind at last abate. The sea became calm. We steamed up the ship channel into the city's upper bay. Abeam of Bedloe's Island and the Statue of Liberty, the refugees stood three and four deep at the port rail, staring. We shortly nosed into a slip at one of Manhattan's North River piers. Our passengers disembarked. They went down the gangway to whatever life their new country held for them.

I look again at the image of the boy in the shallows. I see the red of the shirt, the blue of the shorts. The boy's face is buried in the sea. He seems to be at peace. That, I know, is a delusion. He died hard, I tell you. I could say more. But I've said enough. So I will end this meditation at the place where it began.

We have the ships. We have the crews to sail these ships. We should have sent a ship. That's what I think we should have done.

2017

WHY DO WE TRAVEL?

TRAVEL. The pleasure principle is missing from the word. Its etymology lies in *travail*—hardship, painful effort. The identical spelling in French simply means work. So what impels us to shift ourselves between pinpoints on a map like oversized chess pieces on a stained and battered board?

Libraries are devoted to the notion of travel. Books by the yard tell us what to think about it. I think about it now. And what I think is that those uncounted millions of words in search of an elusive meaning can be condensed into a single aphorism and a related injunction:

"All travel examines an idealized past." That's one. Here is the other: "I can no longer be a tourist in other people's pain."

The first was written by the late Paul Fussell, author and literary critic; the second by a New York newspaperman named Pete Hamill.

Hamill's line cuts closest to the bone. The context was Northern Ireland during a period of sectarian killings. Still, it could

Why Do We Travel?

have been anywhere. From famine to war, from poverty to disease, there are plenty of candidates. Here, for example, is Trinidadian Nobel laureate V.S. Naipaul on the view from an air-conditioned tour bus in the country of his paternal origins, India:

"The unending nullity of the peasant-serf countryside... meandering black rivulets of filth in unpaved alleys," Naipaul writes. He speaks of a population of the impoverished, for whom the aggregate of squalor, misery and disease "no longer had a meaning." It was, he says, "life itself."

What he's talking about by inference is the visitor as voyeur. And so, aware of Naipaul's narrative of horror as well as of Hamill's much-quoted proscription, I would decline to travel to India.

Yet my scruple rings false. It is an intellectual fraud. It is the belated guilt of a wanderer who once traveled with pleasure to more than one country reduced to beggary by the cynicism and oppression of military dictatorships. And in some half-dozen outings to equatorial Africa, I roamed vast plains in search of lion, leopard, elephant. People were not on the menu. For me and others like me, the villages decimated by AIDS and now populated solely by the very young and the very old were out of sight, out of thought.

Like most travelers, I romanticized lost worlds: Plato's Greece; the Egypt of the Pharaohs; Shakespeare's England. In my mind's eye, I had visions of sages in rumpled togas, happy peasants dancing round maypoles.

Winter Passage

Yet what I imagined, I will now tell you, was a theater of the absurd. There was no room in my world view for plague, cruelty, violence, ignorance, lunacy, despair. I had looked with wonder at the great 13th-century cathedrals of France, and at that country's magnificent royal palaces of Chambord and Blois. But if pushed, I think I might have conceded a reluctant truth—I would not have wanted to live in that ancient or medieval past. I was too wedded to my doctors, dentists and indoor plumbing.

So why did I travel? Fear could have had something to do with it. The writer Clive Irving may have got it right when he called travel a rekindling of youth, a species of whistling past the grave. Holding at arm's length the malady of old age.

Or perhaps boredom is the simplest explanation. We escape the humdrum of our lives by joining squadrons of the similarly afflicted to stare at and photograph the ghastly travesties of modern tourism.

In Bavaria, we see apple-cheeked country folk in *dirndl* and *lederhosen*. Or at least that's the stock image of rural Germany. And in Munich we feast on *wurst* and Black Forest cake washed down by foaming steins of the rich, dark local brew. We savor the forced gaiety, the false *gemütlichkeit* of a cavernous, drink-sodden *bierpalast*.

But we are innocent of history. We are unlikely to know that the Nazi concentration camp at Dachau—a genocidal killing ground—is 30 minutes away by train. Local travel brochures, to give them their due, say something about it. You can book a tour.

Why Do We Travel?

Hamburg? Bergen-Belsen, an hour's car journey to the south, is where an estimated 70,000 died of starvation and disease. Berlin? Ravensbrück and Sachsenhausen lie to the north. The killing of Jews and gypsies continued to the final days of the war. And in neighboring Austria, not far from the ski slopes of glittering Salzburg, can be found the Holocaust camps of Ebensee, Gunskirchen, Mauthausen....

And so the question persists. Why do we travel? What do we travel to see?

I give you Salonika, in northern Greece, with its broad, leafy boulevards, its magnificent harbor promenade. The tourist literature speaks with pride of the city's most famous son, Alexander the Great, who won for ancient Greece an empire stretching as far east as India.

But no word will you find about a modern metropolis that once pulsed to the rhythm of Jewish life. Nor is mention made of the atrocities of 1943, when Nazi occupiers bulldozed all but one of Salonika's 36 synagogues and transported a Jewish community of close on 50,000 to the German death camps.

Thus in Salonika, what is it that we have come to see?

Athens, in the south of the country, the capital: a ferroconcrete city of 5 million, half the population of Greece; garbage dumpsters at street corners; refuse and dust blowing in the wind; sidewalks befouled by dogs; the never-ending roar of traffic; the air gray with exhaust fumes; the air, so often trapped in a bowl of surrounding hills, heavy with a blanket of appalling pollution.

Winter Passage

And on a hill dominating the city, the patched, smog-stained remains of an antique temple, its fluted columns and cambered peristyle a poem of balance and symmetry.

Here, like Naipaul in India, we will ride in an air-conditioned bus. We will note in comfort the old temple on its hill, or a palace guard doing balletic high kicks in pleated skirts.

Again the question: what in fact are we looking for? What is the meaning of this place? Is it past or present? If past, precious little of it remains. If it's present, you will, if you look truly, pick out the outline of what for many of its inhabitants has become an unliveable city.

Elsewhere, we have reports from today's new frontiers of tourism:

Turkey: "Terrorist attack at Istanbul nightclub kills 39".... Egypt: "Attack on Coptic cathedral in Cairo kills dozens".... Jordan: "Several security personnel and a Canadian tourist killed in terrorist attack".... Belgium: "Suicide bombers attack Brussels airport".... Germany, Switzerland: "Berlin, Zurich: a day of violence".... Asia: "China choking on smog; Beijing airport shuts down."

And so I ask yet again: why do we travel? Despite the philosophic dictums of Fussell and Irving cited above, I have no good answer. I have no answer at all. The question is rhetorical. It may be unanswerable.

2017

PRODIGAL PADDY—WRITER, WARRIOR, ROGUE

THE year, I recall, was 1992. The sense of place is vivid still. My wife, Caroline, and I had stopped for lunch at a taverna in Kardamyli, a seaside straggle of houses five hours south of Athens by car. Beyond a rim of rocks, the Messenian Gulf glared under a fierce sun. A waiter hovered. My wife—a Greek speaker—translated. I asked about a famous resident, who lived in a cove below the village.

"We see him from time to time," the waiter said. He nodded toward the shore. "He speaks perfect Greek. Better than most Greeks. But you can tell he is not a Greek."

A book published a few months ago in London brought that distant exchange instantly to mind. "Dashing for the Post," edited and annotated by Adam Sisman, is an assemblage of 174 letters written from 1940 to 2010 by the British author, philhellene and war-hero Patrick Leigh Fermor.

Drawn from a far larger hoard, it is an astonishing collection. It brings to life the callow teenager of 1933 who set out to walk

Winter Passage

across Europe and the later writer who produced some of the most luminous travel books in our language.

Paddy, as he universally was known, was a trim, curly-haired adventurer of enormous courage and charm. He was also a sometimes moody, sometimes depressive, sometimes bumptious character addicted to women, alcohol, endless talk and round-the-clock partying. He died in 2011. He was 96.

As his letters make clear, Paddy was an inveterate wanderer who wrote his books in getaways that ranged from Greek islands and French monasteries to a clutch of English hotels and private estates. Critics have judged the bulk of his output—particularly his works celebrating an enduring love affair with Greek culture, landscape and language—to be triumphs of 20th-century literature and scholarship.

The earliest of the letters was written when Paddy was just shy of his 25th birthday. The last two appeared on the same day in 2010, when, as editor Sisman notes, "Paddy was ninety-four...and his voice already hoarse from the throat cancer that would kill him seventeen months later.

"But these letters, like the first and most of the others printed here, exude a zest that was characteristic.... Paddy's letters radiate warmth and gaiety."

Although he was only in his mid-twenties when he penned the initial letter collected by Sisman, the achievement for which he is best known, his walk across Europe, was already behind him. The pair of books he wrote chronicling the first two legs

Prodigal Paddy—Writer, Warrior, Rogue

of his extraordinary trek, "A Time of Gifts" and "Between the Woods and the Water," appeared, respectively, in 1977 and 1986.

A third volume, "The Broken Road," was cobbled together posthumously in 2013 from notes, journals and scraps of manuscript discovered by his biographer, Artemis Cooper, and the travel writer Colin Thubron. Taken as a whole, what emerges from Paddy's works is the image of an unschooled and precocious young voyager who reinvented himself as geographer, antiquarian, ethnologist, speaker of Balkan languages, scholar of classical literature, and historian of art and architecture. Paddy was a lover of beauty and all things of the mind. Above all, he was a peerless storyteller.

Although I traveled frequently to Greece and knew people close to him, I met Paddy only once. The occasion, in 1999, was the talk he gave in Athens honoring an old comrade-in-arms in the World War II battle for Crete, George Psychoundakis. Paddy had commanded several guerilla operations on the German-occupied island, including one of the war's most daring—the ambush and capture of a Wehrmacht general.

Psychoundakis, I noted, was a small, bent, elderly Cretan who leaned for support on a rough-hewn walking stick. As a tough, athletic mountain shepherd in 1943 and 1944, he had run messages to and from Paddy between hideouts in upland caves of the central island. Yet at the Athens tribute, Paddy spoke not about the war but about his old friend's translations

Winter Passage

into Cretan dialect of Homer's "Odyssey" and "Iliad," describing them as formidable feats of erudition and comparative linguistics.

At the time of his talk, Paddy was 84, a solidly built man of middle height. He had a lined, weathered face and an abundant mane of iron-gray hair. Over drinks later that evening, I chatted with him about his stint as a British commando officer operating out of Cairo, where my wife had been born. We talked about his writing, especially his two atmospheric books of Greek travel, "Mani" and "Roumeli." We also touched on a remarkable memoir, "A Time to Keep Silence," which recounted Paddy's various monastic sojourns in France, harbors of refuge that had provided the essential tranquility he needed to think and to work. And we talked about the critically acclaimed volumes thus far published of his European-walk trilogy.

Diffidently, I mentioned the projected third and concluding book. I was uncomfortably aware that Paddy had been laboring on a draft for the better part of a decade.

I could sense at once that I had overstepped. Paddy's mouth tightened in a grimace. He refused to talk about it. The wound of that unfinished text still gnawed. The book obsessed him. And only to people he loved and could trust would he broach the subject of his abortive attempts to complete the manuscript.

In January 2010, Paddy wrote the final letter collected in "Dashing for the Post." The recipient was a dear friend and regular visitor to Kardamyli, Olivia Stewart. Paddy knew he was dy-

Prodigal Paddy—Writer, Warrior, Rogue

ing. "I've managed to do some work," he disclosed, "on the third closing volume of my youthful trilogy.

"I was feeling rather apprehensive about picking it up after a long pause. I've been very worried about this, but to my great relief, the part already written of this last stretch is not nearly as hopeless as I feared it might be, so perhaps it will be OK in the end. I wish my writing had not deteriorated so….Tons of love, Paddy."

And there was a coda: "*Please forgive* this frightfully untidy and *unreadable* letter!"

Please forgive! It was a melancholy refrain that would run through much of his correspondence. In that long-ago year of 1992, shortly after my wife and I had driven from Athens and dined in Kardamyli, I wrote to Paddy to express my admiration for his work.

Many months later—and years before we would meet—a postcard from Greece reached me at my home, in western New York. Paddy's erratic hand was the antithesis of copperplate:

"I'm so sorry answering your kind letter so late," he wrote. "I've been on the move and have only just got back.

"Please forgive?

"Paddy."

1991

SAILING TURKEY'S INDIGO SEA

I SAIL west along the southern shores of Aegean Turkey, where traces of Crusader, Byzantine and Muslim Seljuk settlements sprout like ghosts from the shadow of earlier Greek and Roman ruins.

The Turks call this voyage *mavi yol* (the blue way), a cruise along a remote and unspoiled coast of plunging headlands and sapphire bays.

Haunted by relics of vanished civilizations, it is an enchanted journey, plying the finest—and least known—yachting grounds of the eastern Mediterranean.

*

From the quay of the port city of Marmaris, I board an all-pine motor yacht whose wide beam and flaring bows echo the lines of fishing caiques that have sailed these waters from time beyond memory.

The 60-foot boat is called a *gulet*. Her name is *Melanurya*. She flies the orange-and-blue burgee of a charter-cruise operator.

Sailing Turkey's Indigo Sea

Passing scene on Turkey's Aegean coast—goat ferry to Bozburun.

Melanurya is rigged with a pair of tall masts and a soaring bowsprit. But her Dacron sails are mostly cosmetic. A 140-power Ford diesel will push us along at a more-than-adequate eight miles an hour.

A few feet from the balustraded stern rail is the wheelhouse, with compass, engine controls and a tiny galley containing sink and four-burner propane stove. A shallow stairwell leads forward to six compact double-cabins and two small bathrooms.

As I step aboard, the crew is there to greet me: Ahmet, the captain, in white ducks and blue pullover; Yusef, the dour, dark, full-mustached cook; and Tayfun—he pronounces it "Typhoon"—the tall, fair, clean-shaven deckhand.

It is a few minutes after 9. Yusef and Tayfun haul in the stern

Winter Passage

gangway. The engine coughs. We're away. Marmaris recedes in a narrowing crescent of modern hotels and apartment blocks.

Haze covers the sea. Caiques under sail coast along in a light breeze. I sit on the foredeck watching *Melanurya's* bow dip and rise to the swell. After an hour of cruising, we nose into a high-walled fjord. Below our keel I can see white sand through 20 feet of crystal water.

Ferried by dinghy to shore, I spend an idyllic hour exploring the crumbling apse of a 6th-century Byzantine chapel, then swim back to the *gulet*. Yusef, meanwhile, works culinary magic.

Lunch is a thoroughly Turkish spread of simple ingredients consummately prepared: tomatoes in oil and tangy lamb meatballs accompanied by a fruity white wine from central Anatolia. Like all our meals, it is served alfresco under an awning on the afterdeck.

We anchor before nightfall in a deep bay that is said to have provided refuge for Athenian ships during the Peloponnesian War. I land in the dinghy and climb through a wood of olives to a redoubt of massive stone walls—the great fortress of Loryma—erected by Aegean Greeks more than 2,000 years ago.

From the ramparts, the sea stretches before me to a glittering horizon. Its smooth surface is broken only by the jagged spine of the Greek island of Rhodes, 10 miles to the south.

The next day's dawn is bright and cloudless. I breakfast on olives, feta cheese and a comb of pine-scented honey. Underway with the sun, *Melanurya* rounds the western tip of the Loryma

Sailing Turkey's Indigo Sea

Peninsula and bears east into the Gulf of Yesilova.

The sky is pale. The sea shades to cobalt in the west. Ahead rises an amphitheater of crags cleft by great valleys.

Drifting into a wide tranquil bay, we moor stern first to a seawall backed by lemon trees and a sprinkling of white cottages. Blue and white fishing boats heaped high with nets lie off a shingle beach.

A fisherman tells me in halting English that we have landed at Sogut, and that he has seen fragments of ancient walls high on the slopes of a nearby mountain. According to my map, Sogut lies below the remains of a Greek city that archaeologists call Thyssanos.

From Sogut, we motor south, then double north into a constricted bay. At its head are a mosque, a breakwater, a forest of *gulet* masts: the port of Bozburun.

I land with a fellow passenger, a Turk who speaks flawless English, and trek north across a mile-wide isthmus of shattered rock. Ahmet will bring the boat around Bozburun's western cape to retrieve us from the peninsula's northern shore.

My companion and I pick our way along a stony track flanked by limestone cliffs. The air is pungent with the scent of sage and oregano.

Midway along the gorge, we come upon a gypsy woman draped in yards of red and green cloth. Delicate lines crosshatch her gaunt brown face. The woman stoops to gather the dusty green leaves of the oregano plant. As she does, she speaks rapidly to my companion, who translates:

Winter Passage

"She says she will boil the leaves—we call them *kekik*—to make an aromatic and restorative tea, although she has heard that people in far countries use the herb to flavor meat."

And he adds: "She wishes us good health and a long life."

Ahmet finds us in a fisherman's cove at the mouth of the gorge and not long after sunset we tie up at Selimiye, a straggling row of bars and shops lining a dirt quay. Ashore, I linger over glasses of *raki*, the local aniseed cordial.

Soon it is too dark to walk back through the village to the *gulet*. By prearrangement, Ahmet comes out in the dinghy to take me aboard. I dine on lamb chops, then tumble into bed.

I awake in the morning to the crooning of doves, the bellowing of cows, the plash of fisherman's oars. The sun is hot. The surface of the bay is mirror smooth. There is no wind. Smoke rises straight into the still air from cooking fires. We lie stern first to a small concrete dock, our anchorage rimmed by wild crags.

My head aches from the previous night's *raki*. Yusef, smiling faintly, produces a curative glass of strong, sweetened tea.

We motor north into the Gulf of Hisaronu. We are in a region of vast pine forests. They soften the outlines of crags and promontories. Here and there in this pristine wilderness we see the hint of a stone wall, the trace of an arch.

In a bay called Keci Bucu, we drop anchor 100 meters from the remains of a Crusader castle of the Rhodian Knights of St. John. By mid-afternoon, we shape a course west for the 20-mile run to the popular yachting port of Datca, journey's end.

Sailing Turkey's Indigo Sea

Our route takes us north of the Greek Island of Simi and into the open Aegean. Now the sky becomes veiled with cloud. The sea glints dully, gunmetal gray.

At dusk, we slip through the breakwater at Datca. *Gulets* and sailing yachts crowd the quay. A garland of naked light bulbs illuminates the circular harborside: Bamba Bar, Poppy Bar, carpet and leatherware shops, a yacht provisioner's.

Amplified by loudspeakers atop a nearby minaret, a *muezzin* calls the faithful to prayer. "*Allah-u akbar*," he cries. "God is great."

And through the open door of the Poppy Bar, the voice of Billie Holiday blares back at the *muezzin* a litany of secular sorrow:

"Loverman, oh where can you be?"

2016

THE MAN WHO ATE SQUIRRELS

I WANT to tell you a story. It's about a man I'll call Tom. That was not his real name. For much of his life, Tom had been a dairy farmer in the far western hinterland of New York State, but when I came to know him he was long retired. He lived as a boarder in a gabled, gray-clapboard house in a town a few miles from his home. He was gravely ill.

And as much as the story I have to tell is about Tom himself, it is also about the house where he spent his final days. Those of us who have some connection with the place think of it as a "comfort house," an unusual establishment where people are cared for in the last few weeks or months of their lives.

No more than two of the terminally ill can be accommodated at any one time, and they are called residents, not patients. The house is supported by charitable giving. It offers, without cost to residents or to their families, a clean, airy environment run by a registered nurse with the help of a hundred or so volunteers, people who stand watch in roughly four-hour shifts.

The Man Who Ate Squirrels

The volunteers do sundry jobs. They cook meals. They administer, when needed, under-the-tongue doses of morphine. They keep detailed records of medications, of food and liquids taken or refused—in other words, records of life and eventually of death.

But the main reason volunteers stand watch is to provide companionship. They hold a resident's hand. They smooth a pillow. They reposition a head or a limb. They converse quietly. Occasionally they joke about whatever is likely to raise a smile.

The volunteers are, for the most part, in their 50s and 60s. A few are well past late middle age. A good number of them are widows or widowers, and they come from all walks of life. Some are homemakers. Others are active or retired tradesmen, nurses, doctors, librarians, teachers.

What many of the volunteers experience in their watchkeeping is no doubt what they themselves have had to face. They have cared for husbands, wives or parents; in some cases even for brothers or for sisters.

For most of the volunteers, being employed about the house nourishes a need that many people have to give of themselves. The tasks they perform also force helpers to confront, with whatever reserves of courage they are able to muster, the mystery and universal fear, or terror, of death. The house and its resident occupants provide a necessary framework for attempting to understand and engage with the part of life that is the extinction of life.

My own schedule as a volunteer was, and is, a once-a-week shift. I met Tom in early summer. He lay bedridden, a thin figure,

Winter Passage

in one of the two ground-floor rooms reserved for residents—families are welcome to use a pair of apartments on the upper floor.

Tom talked very little. Yet from time to time as I sat with him, he would speak of his work, years before, as a dairyman farming just short of 300 acres of pasture and arable. He had tended a herd of a few dozen cows, so he talked to me about milk production and the economics of what he did.

One day, out of curiosity, I asked if he, like so many farmers, had been a hunter. His response was matter-of-fact:

"Not deer," he said. "Squirrels."

"Squirrels? What do you do with squirrels?"

"Eat 'em," he said.

"Eat squirrels? You've got to be kidding."

"Very nice," Tom said. "Taste like chicken."

"I ate frog's legs once," I said to him. "I'll give you that much. In France. Not in this country. I wouldn't do it again. The French eat anything. But squirrels? I'm a city boy. I still don't believe it. You're having me on."

The head nurse, a big, stocky fellow in his late 50s, had stopped at the open door. I turned to him. "Have you ever heard of anyone eating squirrels?"

"Absolutely! Wonderful stuff."

"Well, if you can eat squirrels," I said, "what else then? Woodchuck?"

"Excellent," the nurse said, "if you have a young one. Not so

The Man Who Ate Squirrels

good if they're old. Raccoon…."

"No, no." I said, shaking my head. "You cannot eat raccoon."

"Actually not bad," the nurse said. "But they tend to be greasy."

Although propped on pillows and with his eyes half closed, Tom had been listening attentively to the exchange. You could tell he was savoring every bit of it. A small smile played at the corners of his mouth. It was as if—dreaming of the past—he could recall the feasts of game that once had given him so much pleasure.

At the end of summer, a note to house volunteers arrived in my email:

"Tom is continuing on his journey of slowly leaving us."

Family members began to arrive from near and far. Tom died a few days later. He was 93.

2014

THE BROTHERS FROM WICHITA

I'VE been thinking about the Koch brothers. Something I had read brought them to mind. It was a book of medieval history, and it touched on the Latin- and Greek-speaking oligarchs of southern and eastern Europe in the first centuries after the birth of Christ.

The ethos of these particular ancients seemed uncannily to suggest the world view of the pair of ultraconservative Kansas industrialists, Charles and David Koch (pronounced Coke), proprietors of a Wichita-based conglomerate engaged in chemicals, forest products, oil refineries. The company's annual revenues are said to be in the $100-billion range. According to Forbes Magazine, the estimated net personal worth of the brothers exceeds $80 billion.

In addition to their well-documented distaste for current rates of personal and corporate income taxes, the brothers—acting through surrogates—oppose health-care reform and Medicaid expansion. They oppose environmental regulation. They make no secret of their antipathy toward virtually any form of government aid that provides more than minimal assistance to the needy.

There is, ironically, another and less publicized side to the Kochs. Their philanthropies are legion: public broadcasting, hospitals, universities, scholarships, the arts.

And thus the contradiction. I have never been able to fathom why such supremely wealthy men would object to, or feel threatened by, those among their fellow citizens who, for whatever reason, require public support. It cannot be a question of money. After Bill Gates (Microsoft), Warren Buffett (Berkshire Hathaway), and Larry Ellison (Oracle), the brothers are the wealthiest individuals in the United States. They have more money than ever they can possibly use. What, then, is the answer?

Reading historian Peter Brown's brilliant study, "The World of Late Antiquity, AD 150-750," I think I may have stumbled on a clue.

"In any part of the Roman world," writes Brown, the privileged few "found themselves closer to each other than to the vast majority of their neighbors, the 'underdeveloped' peasantry on their doorstep."

It was, he notes, "an aristocracy of amazingly uniform culture, taste and language [that] existed to exclude alternatives to [its] own world." And he adds: "The most blatant feature of this society...was the widening gulf between rich and poor... The prosperity of the Mediterranean world would seem to have

Winter Passage

drained to the top."

Familiar? And so it is possible that the dynastic arrogance of a Marcus Aurelius, a Diocletian or a Constantine has been transmuted in a direct line of descent from 2nd-to-4th-century Rome to the 21st century sociopolitical DNA of the brothers Koch of Wichita, Kansas.

It makes sense. Still, there remains a doubt. It may not be the whole story. It may be too simplistic. Reality perhaps is more subtle. Let me offer a philosophical conjecture.

Through their funding of libertarian policy and advocacy groups, the brothers wield enormous political power. Or at least that is the supposition. But the brothers are old men. As of this writing, one is 79, the other 74. For the old, wealth and power are chimeras. They count in the end for nothing. The brothers are as powerless as the rest of us in the face of inevitable physical decline, powerless to alter the course of what the late surgeon and author Sherwin Nuland laconically called "nature's final victory."

The Kochs are not stupid. They know this. And thus in their political battles, they know also that what they hold in hand are the brittle strands less of power itself than of failing power. They have become, I would argue, actors in a perverse morality play, an allegory of righteousness in which the targets of easy opportunity are government at every level and the poor and indigent supported by government.

That astute observer of American mores, culture and counterculture, Joan Didion, once wrote:

"When we start deceiving ourselves into thinking not that we want something or need something, not that it is a pragmatic necessity for us to have it, but that it is a moral imperative that we have it, then…is when the thin whine of hysteria is heard in the land, and then is when we are in bad trouble."

I suspect she may be right.

1976

FLIGHT

FIVE hours to takeoff. In a basement office at New York's Kennedy International Airport, a British Airways operations officer, Maurice Willson, pores over revised high-altitude weather charts transmitted by wirephoto from the National Weather Service, in Washington.

Fifteen miles away, at the Hotel Berkshire, in New York, pilot John Cross, a stocky man in his early 40's whose hair is beginning to gray at the temples, rests while waiting for the call from Willson that will give him a detailed picture of his responsibilities over the North Atlantic later this winter night.

Willson, meanwhile, surrounded by his weather maps, teleprinters and computer display screens, has been seeking whatever economies in time and fuel he can glean from the vagaries of wind and weather. He looks up at the clock. Just on 7. He picks up the phone and dials Cross's number at the Berkshire. The pilot answers on the first ring. Without preamble, Willson recites the flight plan: in a quiet, toneless voice he ticks off altitude

Flight

(33,000 feet), overwater portion of the route (Gander, Newfoundland, to Shannon, Ireland), takeoff fuel weight (184,000 pounds—enough for 4,000 miles) and fuel to be consumed in flight (136,000 pounds). Estimated flying time is six hours. Distance to destination: 3,025 miles.

"Weather at Kennedy is temp 37, ceiling 2,900 [feet] overcast with 10 miles visibility. Wind is three-one-zero [northwest] at eight knots." The arrival forecast for London's Heathrow Airport is ceiling broken at 1,300 feet, with the wind south of west at 10 knots.

In all of his computations, Willson employs the 6,080-foot nautical mile as the measure of distance; a knot, a measure of speed, is a nautical mile per hour.

"What else can I tell you?" Willson says. "Do you want to stay at 33,000? Yes…I think you're better off. You've got a plus 65 component all the way," he notes, alluding to the mean velocity, in knots, of a high-altitude tail wind, or jet stream. "See you later, then."

*

Aside from a clutch of early arrivals, few passengers have checked in to the terminal. At 7:30, their number increases. In the red-carpeted main-level lounge, they read or chat, or simply doze in their seats.

At 8:40, a chartered bus draws up to a door one level below the passenger lounge. Captain Cross, four gold stripes at his sleeve; David Jevons, 40, his co-pilot, or first officer; and

Winter Passage

29-year-old Andrew Share, the flight engineer, alight first, followed by the cabin staff. The pilots and engineer stand stiff and straight in their dark blue uniforms, with visored caps pulled low over their eyes. They enter a dimly lit corridor and walk to the operations office, where Willson is waiting. There is a subtle tension in their stance; they seem, in a way, unapproachable. They read a copy of their standing orders and study the abstract symbols of wind, fuel weight and engine power before moving off into the night to board the aircraft.

By contrast, the mood of the cabin staff is relaxed, even jocular. The four stewards and nine stewardesses banter with one another in a crew lounge until called to order by their chief, 47-year-old Lawrence Evans, the cabin service officer. A small, wiry man with sharp features and a pleasant smile, Evans looks down at a sheet of paper and begins his briefing: a senior stewardess will have charge of a steward and junior stewardess in first class; the rest of the staff will serve in economy. Evans himself, a 23-year veteran of the line, will roam the entire aircraft.

"The movie is 'The Wind and the Lion,' and it runs for 112 minutes," Evans says. "Standard meal service tonight except for five vegetarian and two kosher. We have 164 passengers in economy, including eight infants and 16 children; 10 in first class."

The payload is 46 percent of capacity, and the cabin staff will have an easy run home. "Right, then," says Evans. "Have a happy trip."

Evans and his staff trek across the tarmac beneath the long,

Flight

wide underbelly of the plane. Close by, under the watchful eyes of flight-engineer Share, the ground crew pumps jet fuel for the flight—aviation-grade kerosene—from underground hydrants into wing tanks.

*

Now 9:15. Passengers file up the terminal's north ramp. They clear the security checkpoint, walk down a jetway and board the aircraft through one of 10 double-width doors. Economy class is a sea of seats, nine abreast, separated by a pair of aisles into rows of three, four and two. The enormous space of Flight 510's interior is reduced to a semblance of scale by partitioned galleys and toilet bays that effectively divide the economy cabin into four compartments.

First class passengers occupy the fifth and narrowest compartment, set in the aircraft's nose below the flight deck, as the cockpit is called. One of the attendants uncorks bottles of champagne. The senior stewardess helps the single V.I.P. in her care, the ballet star Rudolf Nureyev, out of his long brown fur coat, and the dancer walks to the door to watch his fellow passengers board. Near where he stands is a spiral staircase, which leads to the flight deck and to the first-class cocktail lounge.

*

On the flight deck, pilots Cross and Jevons, soon to be joined by Share, hang their caps on snap hooks and place their uniform jackets on hangers in a space to the left of the door. The cockpit is about 12 feet long by seven across, with scarcely more

Winter Passage

than five feet of head room at the pilots' seats. The curved inch-thick windshield is 29 feet above the tarmac. In shirtsleeves, Cross squeezes sideways into the left-hand seat; co-pilot Jevons into the right. Share sits just behind them facing an instrument board crowded with dials and switches that report on and control the plane's vital systems: electrical, hydraulic, oxygen and cabin pressurization. Captain and co-pilot have before and between them control columns and power levers, and the vast array of instruments required to guide and navigate Flight 510. The instrument panel, control column and rudder pedals in front of the co-pilot are twin of the pilot's. Both men have small radar screens at their feet to warn of storms along the track. Emergency oxygen masks are tucked into recesses above their heads.

Share reads aloud from a checklist of control systems and engine start procedures. Cross and Jevons respond, flipping switches—some with test lights—to confirm that their instruments are operating normally. The pilots now perform a critical task: they punch the latitudes and longitudes of Kennedy Airport and checkpoints along the flight paths into the push-button top of the aircraft's inertial navigation system. Housed in the box-like pedestal separating their two seats, the device gauges velocity and directional changes of the aircraft in flight. Through an on-board computer, it displays these changes in the form of a running digital readout of location and speed.

Cross and Jevons actively fly the plane only on takeoff and

Flight

landing. With Share, they will spend the rest of their time recording information provided by the array dials. They will keep a visual and radar watch for other aircraft. They will radio periodic position reports to ground control stations and receive and analyze weather data. And they will stay alert for the flashing light or tell-tale flicker of an instrument needle that warns of a malfunction. The hour-by-hour job of maintaining course and altitude, however, will be left to the autopilot, whose gyroscopes—linked to the inertial navigator—correct drift from a set heading by adjusting the plane's controls.

*

The pilots and the flight engineer strap on their shoulder harnesses. Cross reaches for the start levers, on the center pedestal below the throttles. One at a time, he brings the engines to life. The four Pratt & Whitneys catch with a resonant whine. The turbine-powered compressors pump air into the combustion chambers, mixing it with vaporized fuel.

The boarding door thuds shut. One of the ground crew kicks the chocks clear of the wheels and a tow truck drags the aircraft backward. The truck unhooks, and now the Boeing moves forward under its own power. The plane sways and jostles along the taxiway.

The cabin attendants take up stations in the aisles to demonstrate the use of oxygen masks and life jackets, and they point to where the life rafts are stowed. They do this mechanically, as if engaging in a faintly distasteful task. The aircraft bumps over

Winter Passage

tar seams. The taxiway is lined with cobalt-blue lights.

An extraordinary calm pervades the cockpit. The pilots' faces are expressionless in the soft light from the instrument panel. Clustered before each of the two men are radio and barometric altimeters, compasses, a course deviation indicator, an airspeed indicator, an artificial horizon, and a clock set to London time (five hours ahead). Centered on the console are four columns of glowing dials that monitor the engines' exhaust pressure (thrust) and temperature, air-compressor revolutions, and fuel flow. The autopilot engage-switch and inertial navigator display-screens are on the cowling at the top of the panel.

Cross and Jevons check their instruments. The pilots' earphones emit a filtered, crackling sound: "Five-one-oh cleared for takeoff on 31 left. Wind is three-two-zero…15 knots." The time: 10:20.

With a steady motion, Cross pushes the four throttles forward to full thrust. The aircraft accelerates. Jevons's eyes are fixed on the airspeed indicator. In 25 seconds, as runway lights flash by, the indicator needle touches 130 knots and Jevons says "V-1," the speed that relates aircraft weight and momentum to runway length: if an engine fails before V-1, Cross still has plenty of runway left in which to brake to a halt; beyond V-1, he must, and can, commit the plane to flight despite an engine loss.

But Flight 510's engines are running smoothly, and at 140 knots, when Jevons calls out "Rotate," Cross eases back on his elevator-aileron control column, "rotating," or lifting, the air-

Flight

craft's nose upward. The 300-ton, 231-foot-long plane speeds along the runway in this attitude, nose up, the rush of air across and below the curved airfoil of the wings imparting upward suction, or lift; and at 150 knots, Cross pulls back on the column. The plane rises into the night sky. Cross soon shifts control to the autopilot and Flight 510 settles on a northeast heading in a slow, steady climb in the direction of Boston.

*

As the plane passes from calm air to the eastward-flowing jet stream, invisible currents bump it lightly, then more violently. Crockery crashes to the floor in one of the galleys. Soon the shocks subside. Thirty-seven minutes into the flight, the aircraft reaches its cruising altitude of 33,000 feet, over Boston, and Boston air-traffic controllers clear the plane for the next leg of the journey, on a northeast course to Moncton, New Brunswick.

The motion of the aircraft has lulled the infants to sleep. Their bassinets are clipped to the partition bulkheads. The first dinner trays emerge from the electric warming ovens. The single menu in economy class consists of pot roast, vegetables and a side dish of smoked salmon. Plastic dishes and cups. Pepper and salt in corrugated paper containers.

In first class, the fold-back seat trays have been set with starched linen and gleaming crystal. The attendants serve each course separately on Royal Doulton bone china. The starter is chilled Iranian caviar followed by a choice of pheasant in wine and brandy sauce or pan-fried brook trout with capers and

Winter Passage

shrimp. Wines of excellent vintage accompany the meals. The dishes are cleared away, and a new service is laid: ripe Stilton in a jar. And Cockburn's Special Reserve Port.

Two hours into the flight, the lights in economy and first class dim, as in a theater, and ceiling projectors switch on at four stations. Camels galloping across the desert. The aircraft races through the night.

Flight deck of a British Airways Boeing 747.

Flight

*

Flight 510 is surrounded by inviolate air space. No other aircraft may intrude on the section of sky that encases it like a cocoon. But Flight 510 is also a prisoner of this circumscribed world of compass heading and altitude. The plane may not deviate from its pre-filed flight plan without first getting the approval of ground control points along its route. Moncton has by now cleared Flight 510 for Gander, and the aircraft's course begins to flatten out to the east. Two hours and 20 minutes into the flight, past Gander, the tail wind drops. Flight 510 has been testing the lower boundary of the stratosphere in a region called the tropopause, where the jet stream lives. But now the tropopause is rising, and the tail wind rises with it. Cross radioes Gander Oceanic Control, which has jurisdiction to the 30th meridian of longitude—halfway across the North Atlantic—requesting permission to climb from 33,000 to 37,000 feet. Gander acknowledges. The aircraft rises to find the wind. At 37,0000 feet the wind blows fair and Flight 510 makes good a ground speed of 590 knots: 680 miles per hour.

*

Cross has flown for the line 18 years: in jumbo jets since they entered service, in 1970; before that in Boeing 707's and Comet 4's. He is slow of speech, but possessed of unquestioned authority. Jevons, with the line 17 years, is soon to be made captain; and Share, the youngest of the three, has been flying for five years.

Winter Passage

Now, hunched over their instruments, the pilots and the engineer record evidence of progress toward an invisible horizon adduced from dials and gauges. In the darkened cockpit, without visual reference points, there is no sense of motion; there is only the sound of air rushing across the windshield and aluminum skin—it hisses like live steam.

*

Far over the open ocean, in the gulf of night, the aircraft appears frozen in time and space. Flight seems to be a conjurer's trick, an entrancing illusion, and the cockpit no more than a dreamy domestic scene. Briefcases and loose leaf binders are scattered about. There are cups of tea or coffee. Jevons momentarily rests his forehead against one hand. Share, like a schoolboy doing his sums, enters rows of figures in one of his logs. Cross props an elbow on the back of his seat; his left hand grasps a small metal grip above the windshield. A steward enters, hands Cross yet another cup of tea, which the pilot transfers carefully to the shelf at his side. The men say little to one another.

Suddenly Jevons points ahead and to his right. "Look." A thin silver horn rises in the southeastern sky. Cross stares at the moon and says, without affectation, "That's one of the glories of flying."

On the instrument console, a digital readout reels off changes in the aircraft's latitude and longitude. Amber electronic counters in front of both pilots now register a ground speed of 547 knots—air speed and tail wind combined—and distance to the

Flight

next course change. Three hours into the flight, the plane banks, steadies on a new heading. The moon climbs higher.

*

The movie ends three hours and 30 minutes into the flight. Passengers drift off to sleep beneath a jumble of blankets. A man paces to and fro, hugging and shushing a restless child. The arms of children hang to the floor and sway gently as the aircraft strikes turbulence. In the lighted galleys, the cabin attendants stand easy, smoking, conversing softly.

*

The cockpit crew is silent, lost in a reverie of instruments. Four hours and 20 minutes into the flight, there is in the east a faint abating of the dark. Soon light breaks upon the horizon in waves of burnt orange, saffron, emerald. A blanket of stratocumulus shields the ocean from view. Share moves his seat forward to converse with Cross. The pilot, in what has become a characteristic attitude, grips the handhold at his left. His eyes stay fixed on the instrument panel. As Flight 510 consumes fuel and becomes lighter, the airspeed creeps up to the giant Boeing's design limits; and the throttles—not linked to the autopilot—must be retarded manually. Cross jiggles each of the knuckled levers in turn with a thumb and forefinger until the instruments display readings that satisfy him. Four hours and 40 minutes into the flight, one of the digital panels shows that the aircraft is 172 nautical miles west of Shannon, where the next course change will take place.

Winter Passage

One, two…four vapor trails appear like red scars on the eastern horizon. Airliners converging on the Shannon check point. Cross fiddles with his radar, and Ireland's scalloped coast is projected onto the screen. Although the sun has not yet risen, the roseate hue in the east gives way to a band of white light. Jevons polishes his sunglasses. The clouds below are deeply contoured hills and valleys.

*

Light suffuses the passenger compartments. As on a ship, the work of landfall begins. The attendants clatter about in the galleys preparing a breakfast of juice, pastry and coffee. Children sit up and rub their eyes. Queues form at the aircraft's 11 toilets.

*

Five hours into the flight, the sun breaks through the cloud cover. Cross, Jevons and Share adjust their shoulder harnesses. Share makes notations on a pad and passes a bit of paper to Cross. The pilot, still gripping his window handhold, not wearing sunglasses, squints to left and right and then left again. He quickly scans his instruments, and twisting in his seat, the instruments on Share's console, too. Share begins calling off items in a pre-descent checklist. Like priests muttering a litany, Cross and Jevons respond. The instrument needles are boldly white against black backgrounds. The sun is strong. Long glancing rays poke into recesses of the cockpit. Radar sweeps the horizon.

*

At five hours and 30 minutes into the flight, the nose of

Flight

the aircraft suddenly dips. The altimeter needle unwinds like a child's toy. Flight 510 is dropping at the rate of 5,000 feet a minute. Guided by the autopilot—neither Cross nor Jevons touches the controls—the rate of the descent slows; the plane pulls level at 10,800 feet, then begins to sink again, but more gradually. Unseen below the clouds, Ireland drifts by. Flight 510 heads out over St. George's Channel and cuts the Welsh coast at Strumble Head. The altimeter reads 7,000 feet. Beads of water seep from the emergency roof hatch, at the rear of the cockpit. They collect in a rivulet and splatter on Cross's arm. The pilot's concentration is absolute; he seems not to notice. Flight 510 descends eastward on a line to Reading and London. England, like Ireland and Wales, lies hidden beneath a mantle of gray.

Five hours and 45 minutes into the flight, the main landing gear—16 wheels on four massive supports—and the dual-wheel nose gear rumble down into position. South of Heathrow Airport, Cross disengages the autopilot. With gentle pressure on control column and rudder pedals, he brings the giant plane round in a wide left turn. He will land to the west. But now in cloud, Cross's visibility is nil. He aligns a gun-sight type of instrument on signals transmitted by a runway radio beacon. At 2,000 feet, Flight 510 emerges in the clear. Below, green fields and blocks of flats. Runway 28 rushes up to meet the plane. Airspeed: 136 knots.

Six hours into the flight, the tires squeal on asphalt. Throttle levers back. Hinged plates called spoilers—air brakes—pop up

Winter Passage

from the wings. The aircraft slows. Flight 510 rolls along a taxiway to its terminal bay. Cross shuts down the engines. It is a dull, drizzly morning in London.

The passengers disembark. Cross and his crew leave the aircraft, file their reports, then disperse to their homes.

1975

ENCOUNTER IN PARIS

HIS was the only table with a chair left vacant, and I begged permission, addressing him in French.

"Please," he said, in English. "You honor me."

He was thin and stooped. He had a small mustache and graying hair. His head and hands shook slightly, in the manner of sick people and drinkers.

"I apologize for my poor accent," I said.

"My dear boy," he said. "It is not a question of accent. One knows the French immediately. They have hubris. Would you not say so?"

I said it was something I had not thought about.

"It is unnecessary to think about," he said. "They are a disgusting people. Still," he added, "I am quite at home in Paris."

The waiter came and I ordered soup and a glass of wine. The restaurant was comfortably warm. On this autumn day—the year was 1960—it had been raining, but was not now, and people could be seen through the darkening windows hastening

Winter Passage

to their destinations. Chestnut pushcarts with smoking braziers stood nearby at the *carrefour* and in front of the Café Rotonde there were wooden stalls of oysters, clams and spiny sea-urchins.

"I am a creature of habit," the man across the table was saying. "I prefer no other city, but I leave with first frost. I go to St. Moritz. Do you ski?"

"Unfortunately, no."

"You must try. It is a matter of coordination. It has always been my great solace. My doctors have warned me not to ski. But I am going to confound them." He bent forward and pulled back the hair from his brow, exposing a thin purple scar. "I wear a bit of tin plate," he said.

"I am sorry."

"A treacherous road," he said. "A remembrance of Spain. Between Girona and Sant Feliu...."

"It is none of my business, of course," I said. "Possibly your doctors are right."

He gestured dismissively. "The doctors know nothing. It is only the money that interests them. But the money is nothing."

"It is something for many people."

He shrugged. "If it pleases you to think so. The money itself is nothing. My mother had a great deal of it....*Chère maman*...." And he fell silent, eating slowly, his head quivering now and again.

"Well," he said, raising a hand for the waiter. "I hope you will attempt skiing. I assure you, it is an excellent and salubri-

Encounter in Paris

ous sport. Whatever you do, though, do not go to Davos. The atmosphere there is inflexible. At the better hotels, one is not permitted to dress casually for dinner."

The waiter came and made the addition.

"Remember. You might consider Zermatt. But do not go to Davos."

"I will take your advice," I said.

*

I did not see him in the quarter again that winter. I did not see him at all until late in the spring, and then by chance. It was early one Sunday morning and the sun was bright and warm. I had been walking along the Boulevard Montparnasse where it intersects with the Rue Chevreuse when he fell into step beside me.

"How are you?" I said. "How was St. Moritz?"

He tapped the plate in his head and smiled. "Magnificent! Did I not tell you? Those stupid doctors know nothing. The skiing was first rate and I have never felt better."

His head trembled as he spoke, but his pallor had given way to a fragile, almost roseate, glow.

"And you?" he said. "Did you take my advice? Were you in Zermatt?"

"I disappoint you. I have barely stirred from the quarter."

"*Tant pis*—too bad—but no matter," he said. "There will be another time."

He suggested a promenade. I did not mind; I had no other

Winter Passage

plan. At the statue of Balzac, we turned down the Boulevard Raspail and walked under the tall trees with the sun falling through the new leaves and dappling the walk. We strolled along the boulevard to where it debouches onto the Boulevard St. Germain and then past the Assemblée and onto the broad expanse of the Pont de la Concorde. From the cambered walkway midpoint on the bridge, I could see before me the grand symmetry of the adjoining square and its obelisk, and beyond, the Rue Royale and the Madeleine, and very white in the distant clear air on a hill above the city the domes of Sacré-Coeur.

We crossed the bridge and walked down the steps onto the quay along the river. There were fishermen dozing in the sun but no fish in their catch baskets. Refuse floated with the current; yet the Seine had a clean, strong smell, like that of creosote.

We walked under the bridge, where the clean smell turned sour in the deep, dank shade, then emerged squinting in the bright light. Off to the left of the quay was a ramp that led down to the river's edge. It was there that we sat down to rest.

My companion pointed toward the somnolent fishermen. He had suddenly become dour. "Look at them," he said. "They don't have two sous to rub together. Yet nothing bothers them. How I envy their ease."

I wondered why he should envy the fishermen, as he had been to St. Moritz, and they, I should say, had not. But I said nothing.

"*Chère maman* had a fine big house," he went on, as though

Encounter in Paris

in response to my unspoken question. "We lived in America, in Newport, on Bellevue Avenue, if the name means anything at all to you. Life there was a curiosity. In summer you arose and went riding or swimming. The régime did not vary. You changed for tennis. You showered before luncheon. In the afternoon you changed again for cocktails. And then of course you changed for dinner. *Maman,* flitting about like a butterfly, chattering foolishly: 'Hurry up, hurry up, have you got on a clean shirt? Oh, do hurry, we shall be late.'"

His head trembled and he smiled thinly.

"It was a life exhausted of all content, a snob's life. I would not want to live it over again. Activity. Pointless, pointless. What I have been seeking is peace. I desire to be by myself and to have peace."

"It is peaceful here," I said

"It is not the same thing," he said. "I do not have any peace."

"Perhaps it was your injury."

He shook his head. "I lack tranquility. I did not enjoy myself at St. Moritz. I lied to you. I did not enjoy the skiing." He paused. "I am boring you."

"Not at all," I said.

"There is nothing to be done," he said. "It is a matter of upbringing. *Chère maman*—she dragged me with her from pillar to post. She was a compulsive traveler. Deauville. Cannes. Cap d'Antibes. Klosters. Vevey. Rapallo. Estoril." He smiled as at a dimly remembered joke. "I assure you there is no levity in

Winter Passage

my mirth. We were contemptible. We had no dignity. We were treated with disdain. Wine waiters, table waiters, head waiters, bowing and scraping with those terrible smiles, rubbing their hands and bobbing up and down and cupping their hands behind their backs, awaiting payment for servile insolence."

He looked away, across the river, toward the rooftops and chimney pots of the opposite bank. A Dutch barge, long, clean, deeply laden, passed in mid-Seine, pushing up a bow wave. For a time, he watched the vessel's progress. It moved rapidly downstream toward the Pont Alexandre Trois. The gilt statuary atop the four massive pillars of the bridge coruscated in the sun. He addressed me again. He told me he went to Nice each year, in the spring, to put flowers on his mother's grave. He would leave for the south the following week and stay the summer on the Côte d'Azur.

The sun on the quay had become very warm. He invited me to take a beer with him at a nearby café, but I declined. We shook hands and I watched him walk off.

I left the city soon after to begin a different existence. The last time I saw him, he was sitting alone at a table on the terrace of the Café Coupole, on the Boulevard Montparnasse. He waved a greeting to me, but as I had an engagement, I could not stop. I hurried on, and we did not speak.

2017

THE SAILOR WHO LONGED FOR A HERO'S DEATH

I MET a man in Trieste. He idled on the harbor quay a few paces from a sea-stained cruising yacht. His stance was meditative. Still, you could tell he was not a tourist. The man belonged to that boat, and he surely looked the part: an antique of a mariner, one of the breed of ocean nomads sailing their little ships wherever the wind would blow them. The boat flew the British flag.

Years later, browsing the dollar discard bin of a New York bookstore, I picked up a yachting memoir. It had an appealing title—"Oyster River." Though I was addicted to anything literary that had to do with the sea, I had heard of neither book nor author.

As I began leafing through the pages, I came up sharp. The dedication startled me. I knew that name: "To the late Vice-Admiral Sir Malcolm Lennon Goldsmith…with love, esteem, and gratitude."

This was the clue that led me in time to unravel the bizarre

Winter Passage

story of the old man I had met on the quay in Trieste.

George Millar, the book's author, was a Scottish adventurer cut from the same imperial Britannic cloth as the admiral he had once befriended. Beginning at war's end, Millar had embarked on a string of deepwater European yacht voyages that resulted in three classic sailing narratives. "Oyster River," last in the series, appeared in 1963.

The tale I want to tell, though, dates from a decade earlier. It was the summer of 1953. I had a billet then in a merchant ship calling at Mediterranean ports. We had tied up in Trieste behind an ungainly little sailing yacht. I judged her length to be not much more than 30 feet. In the style of Greek fishing caiques, she had a pair of eyes painted at the bows. The name stenciled below the cap rail on her stern quarter was *Diotima*.

Ashore along the quay, I fell into conversation with the boat's master. He called himself Goldsmith. He was of middle height, bearded, with angular, chiseled features. His face and arms had been burnt bronze by the sun. I put his age at 70, maybe a bit older. He told me he'd arrived in Trieste after hard passages from England, the West Indies and Malta. He was bound east for Greece. Though he didn't talk about it, I had the impression he was short of everything from cash to food. I liberated a sack of oranges from my ship's galley, and the sailor invited me aboard his boat for a drink.

A woman sat in the cockpit. She was thin and reedy—as weathered as the master. I clambered down from the quay

The Sailor Who Longed for a Hero's Death

and followed the two of them into the yacht's cabin. It was small, dark, oppressive. The woman—her name was Margaret Adam—poured measures of gin and lime. Lacking refrigeration, we drank them warm. We yarned about ships and seafaring and about ports we knew. Soon it was time for the old man's nap, and I left. My ship sailed the next morning. I never saw them again.

For years, I thought no more about *Diotima* and her skipper until that day when I stumbled on Millar's book. In a note to the author, I related my long-ago encounter with the yacht's master and mate.

His response was immediate:

"I have been too busy to answer letters. Yours is very interesting.

"I loved Admiral Goldsmith very deeply from the moment I first met him aboard *Diotima* in Gibraltar. I found his voice and personality and his practical-cum-romantic attitude to the sea and life quite irresistible. He was a man whom you either hated or loved and thank you for being kind to him and for those oranges."

Millar went on:

"Admiral Goldsmith died in 1955 aboard *Diotima,* in Greece. He was determined to die in Greek waters. He and Margaret Adam, the companion you met him with, were just casting off from the quay at Turco Limano, the yacht harbor near Piraeus, when he expired. Heart trouble. She had the greatest bother getting the Greeks to accept the body ashore, but eventually they

Winter Passage

did after being pressed by the British ambassador and on being told that Goldsmith was a famous English sailor and a noted Grecophile. He is buried at Athens.

"Margaret, a London spinster, was the only person he would sail with latterly. She was very good to the old boy, and my wife and I are grateful to her for making his last years go as he wished.

"*Diotima* was probably the worst design ever to come off a drawing board. She was a dreadful vessel, slow, ugly, overheavy everywhere. Goldsmith had retired after a fine career in the Royal Navy, but in 1939 he rejoined of course and led some of the most dangerous and most costly convoys, both to Russia and, worse still, to Malta. They tell me he was an inspiring but terrifying leader, because he always wanted 'Nelson's death,' i.e., in action on his quarterdeck.

"He was a 'bad' husband. After the war he gathered what money he could lay hands on and abandoned Lady Goldsmith, building *Diotima* and skipping off in mid-winter with one daughter and her friend, Miss Adam. They ran straight into severe southwest gales in the Bay of Biscay, and after a real towsing put into Vigo, where the daughter suddenly decided to fly away. Margaret stayed, and that was how their rather odd, but immensely successful, association began.

"If you visited the yacht you must have interested or amused him, because he was ruthless with bores. Once in Gibraltar, he was having tea with us when a rather distinguished Eng-

The Sailor Who Longed for a Hero's Death

lishwoman came to call with some friends, and with a cry of 'painted women!' the admiral sprang for the shore over 8 feet of oily water.

"He hailed from Dartmouth, in England's West Country, and prior to *Diotima* he owned three finer yachts and did noted cruises across the Atlantic and in the Aegean. Once, when posted to be Commander of the Dockyard, Malta, he decided to sail a newly built cutter, *Rame,* direct there from Dartmouth without stops, single-handed. He ran into calms in the western Mediterranean and began to go off his head, throwing the spoons overboard and carefully stowing the trash in a drawer. Later, Lady Goldsmith wished to settle in Lymington, a pretty and civilized little Georgian yachting town, which the admiral loathed. He bought her a house in a row and called it Deadly Nightshade."

And Millar added, in laconic tribute: "There are very few like him."

2016

WHATEVER HAPPENED TO KERNAN?

NOT long ago, a line in a British weekly caught my eye. "An agreeable rendezvous for departed shades." The writer was talking about death notices. It set me to thinking about how people read newspapers. In my own case, for example, I shun the front page. Now that I've grown older, I turn immediately to the obituaries—people I once knew, people I've known by reputation, people I've managed to outlast.

A friend in Boston recently sent me one of these obits. It arrived in response to a casual phone conversation. "By the way," I'd said to my friend, "whatever happened to Kernan?"

Now, there are plenty of Kernans in the Boston phone directory. But my friend and I are of a certain age. The Kernan we recalled was that singular character of five or six decades ago: Reginald Kernan—the Kernan of the elite Milton Academy for boys and of Harvard Medical School; the Kernan who, against all the odds of rational behavior, had chucked doctoring to reinvent himself as a European film star.

Whatever Happened to Kernan?

And thus the obituary, from The Boston Globe. Kernan was dead.

I knew Kernan. I'd met him in Paris, where I worked on a newspaper. That was in the early 1960s. At the beginning of the decade, I'd quit a reporter's job at one of the Boston dailies to live in France. Kernan, coincidentally, had once had a stint as a novice sportswriter on the same New England broadsheet, The Traveler.

Thus it was a Traveler editor who, in the spring of 1961, telephoned with an appeal to track down the budding actor—the editor remembered him as "that tall, skinny kid wandering around in a kind of dream"—and cable back a feature on why a onetime pediatrician would make a mid-life course correction from medicine to movie making.

I found Kernan in a dubbing studio on the Champs-Élysées, the main boulevard of central Paris. Co-starring opposite the French cinema-idol Simone Signoret in "Les Mauvais Coups" ("Hard Knocks"), he was recording a couple of audio sequences before leaving for Italy to shoot the final scenes.

Even in the darkened studio, the 45-year-old actor was hard to miss. At six-foot-six and a near-twin of Gregory Peck, he stood staring at his gangling image on a wide screen—a tall man in a raincoat walking in a winter landscape studded with bare, black trees. The camera panned to a flock of crows.

Kernan's character raises his shotgun. He fires twice. A crow falls, hops wounded across a field. Kernan grips the wrong end

Winter Passage

of the gun. Using it as a club, he smashes at the crow.

"That was a great day," he told me after I had introduced myself. "I killed twelve. I was supposed to be sore at Simone, who plays my wife, and I go on killing crows. I beat one to death and fling it into her room."

The director, hovering nearby, said something to Kernan. The actor began to breathe into a microphone, coordinating rhythm and sound-volume to his likeness stalking across the screen. After he had repeated the process a few times, we left the building and crossed the Champs-Élysées.

We walked up the boulevard to Fouquet's, a popular hangout for people in the arts. Kernan ordered a dozen oysters, steak, a half-liter of wine. Through the terrace windows we could see strollers wandering by in the warm sun.

As he ate, Kernan talked about his past. He spoke of his Boston boyhood and of the boarding school he had attended, in suburban Milton. He told me about his medical education at Harvard, the general practice he had opened and his subsequent service in the Army Medical Corps. He told me about his crowning professional achievement—a staff appointment in pediatrics and internal medicine at the celebrated American Hospital, in Paris.

But something had happened in Paris. In 1958, the hospital rescinded the Bostonian's appointment. The incident—an undisclosed administrative dispute —was to have ironic and lasting consequences.

Whatever Happened to Kernan?

To continue to practice medicine as an American in Paris, Kernan would have had to retain the affiliation. But for whatever reason, reinstatement appeared unlikely. Kernan was in a quandary. He wanted to stay in medicine; he wanted to stay in Paris. Finally, broke and reduced to sleeping in his car, he began to pick up modeling work.

"I hated it," Kernan told me. "But I was in trouble and needed a living. I did ads for Air France. I did ads for De Beers diamonds. I even once did an ad for a hemorrhoid remedy because no other model would touch it."

A friend had heard that "Les Mauvais Coups" was seeking the male lead. The friend recommended Kernan—who spoke fluent French—to the director. The director liked him. Simone Signoret liked him. But could he act? Screen tested, he turned out to be the man they were looking for.

In the film, Kernan plays an American race-car driver married to a Frenchwoman. The movie is about the disintegration of their marriage. Following release in France, it would be screened in American theaters as "Naked Autumn."

Kernan told me he had got into acting solely to make money. He led an agreeable bachelor's existence in an ancient riverside quarter of Paris. The Seine flowed placidly by his window. He numbered among his neighbors the American novelist James Jones and the French artist Marc Chagall.

Still, he said, he had every intention one day of going back to medicine. "It wouldn't be hard for me to pick up where I'd left

Winter Passage

off. A switch in careers like this hasn't been easy. Medicine was certainly more satisfying.

"But one has to be adaptable. This is new. You're going to live….how long? Seventy years?

"So you do new things. Why not?"

More than half a century after I had had this exchange with the doctor-turned-actor, I opened the yellowing obituary notice my friend had sent from Boston. It was dated 1983. Kernan didn't make it to 70. Twice married, he died in Paris at 68.

The obituary said he had acted in a few more French films and worked from time to time as a journalist.

He never returned to medicine.

1996

AFOOT IN EUROPE'S HIGH COUNTRY

WE were a group of reasonably fit and determined ramblers trekking south with our guide across a remote alpine wilderness.

For the next seven days, traveling single file and at one point roped together on dangerously steep terrain, we would roam ridges and upland valleys falling to the joint frontiers of France, Italy and Switzerland.

The late-spring outing, when snow still clogged the high passes, would cover the length of one of the world's most demanding hiking trails: the 70-mile circuit of Mont Blanc—central peak in the wall of rock that divides northern Europe from the Mediterranean Sea.

The journey would take us to elevations of up to 10,000 feet, with nights spent in clean but spartan inns and mountain refuges. And as in so many ventures that challenge body and spirit, the trek, though exhilarating, would become in the end a test of endurance, a test of self: as much a random exploration of our

Winter Passage

inner landscapes as it was of the rugged grandeur of crag and snow.

First Day: We meet our guide in Chamonix, the French ski and hiking center shadowed by the white-capped dome of Mont Blanc, highest peak in Europe. He is Jean-Marie Olianti, a senior member of the team of professional mountaineers known as the Compagnie des Guides de Chamonix.

There are four in our party: a young woman from Brittany, a couple from Paris and myself, the sole American. For the span of the trip we will converse in a serviceable mix of French and English.

Jumping-off point for the trek is the upland village of Les Houches, reached by a gondola lift just outside Chamonix. We begin with a deceptively easy descent on springy paths. Jean-Marie, lean and weather-beaten, strides ahead at a rhythmic pace, natural gait of the mountain man. In mid morning, he gestures toward a far-off pass.

"That's where we stay tonight," he says. "Maybe another six, seven hours." In the Alps, he notes, distance is always measured in time.

As we climb now onto higher ground the going gets tougher. The sun is hot, the air windless. Four hours into the walk, with calves starting to cramp, we slip our packs—they hold water bottles, lunch provisions, a change of clothes—and find respite from the trail in the shade of a wood. We snack on sausage and dark peasant bread.

Afoot in Europe's High Country

Surrounded by glacier-clad mountains, alpine hikers trek along the joint frontiers of France, Italy and Switzerland.

Soon on the march again, we toil up a gorge with a stream plunging on our right. In late afternoon, we come out onto a plateau flanked by peaks and ridges that tower above us like shattered teeth.

The path twists uphill through meadows to a 6,000-foot saddle and the first of our overnight stops. The Chalet de la Balme is fairly typical of its type, a concrete building of mixed-sex dormitories with bunk beds and flush toilets. In an adjacent dining room the evening meal is plain but ample: turkey, cheese and wine.

Second Day: I don a fleece jersey against the cold, breakfast on bread and tea and am on the trail by 7. Shafts of sunlight bathe a wildly magnificent amphitheater of peaks, gleaming

Winter Passage

white above green valleys.

Hiking south, we climb into snow fields. Their reflected glare reddens the skin and dazzles the eye. We doff jerseys, apply sun block, put on dark glasses. The uphill walk is punishing. But we are rewarded at every rise by tremendous views of snowy mountains and of waterfalls plummeting from the high crevasses.

By mid afternoon we gain a 9,000-foot pass, the Col des Fours, and run, slide and boot-ski downhill through packed snow. We leap across a brook on the valley floor. Soon afterward, as the sun dips below the ridges, we reach our scheduled refuge.

Les Mottets, a converted cow shed, is short on privacy and comfort. Bedding is aligned cheek-by-jowl on a 50-foot platform; the bathroom is a quaint anachronism of squat toilets. But the food that night is hearty and delicious: beef stew washed down with pitchers of rough French red wine drawn from the barrel.

Third Day: We hike northeast into the sun. Glaciers fall gray as elephant hide behind us. In four hours of grueling uphill work, we reach our first objective, the 8,300-foot Seigne Pass. A brass plaque pointing north to "Monte Bianco"—the peak soars above us to a height of more than 15,000 feet—is our sole reminder that we have crossed the frontier into Italy.

From the pass, we lope downhill to the Veni Valley, then begin the inevitable afternoon climb, this time a five-hour traverse of aprons of snow. We are surrounded by a world of snow and sun. Above us glisten icy crags. Below lie dizzying chasms. Turning the crest of a ridge, we amble down through pastures to the Maison Vielle, a handsome mountain inn with a dormitory of double bunks above a stone-flagged dining room.

The evening meal is consummately prepared: pasta and veal scallopine accompanied by a full-bodied wine, a Barbera d'Asti, from southern Italy.

Fourth Day: We trek down 2,000 vertical feet to Courmayeur, a pretty little resort town of chalets and cobbled streets; and after a brief rest begin slogging up the southern slope of a 7,500-foot peak, Monte della Saxe.

Once more, the climb is interminable. After a draining day, as lengthy as the one that preceded it, we reach our destination—the Bertone refuge—perched thousands of feet above the Ferret Valley of neighboring Switzerland.

In a bare dining room of trestle tables, we dine sumptuously on polenta, sausage and goat cheese, washed down yet again with a robust red wine from the barrel.

Fifth Day: We hike into Switzerland at the Ferret pass and in a few hours veer west to the boulder-strewn and snow-filled Arpette Valley, the route back to France.

We reach a chalet-style inn, the Relais d'Arpette, long before sundown. It has the usual double bunks, but also that most welcome of amenities, a sparkling modern bathroom.

Sixth Day: Ascending the Arpette, we run for the first time into trouble. The snow slope ahead rises at a daunting angle. But it is our

Winter Passage

only route to the next pass, a distant notch between two crags.

Jean-Marie makes us fast to a nylon rope. He hauls the loose end a hundred feet uphill. Cautiously we climb after him.

Part way up the slope, I let my gaze wander from the path. Instantly I slip and go down. But the tether holds—without it there would have been a thousand-foot slide to boulders below.

It takes us three hours of relentless effort to reach the pass, where we slump exhausted against a rock. My right knee, twisted in the fall, has begun to stiffen.

Later, as I limp toward our evening stop, an inn at the foot of the great Trient Glacier, Jean-Marie offers to carry my 20-pound pack on top of his own much heavier one. I decline.

"Are you sure?" he says. I am not sure at all, but I motion him on.

Seventh Day: We are on the home stretch. In a cooling drizzle, first of the outing, we tramp south to the French border at the 7,200-foot Balme Pass. We can make out, far below, toy-like villages and the sprawl of Chamonix under the loom of Mont Blanc.

We scramble down on loose gravel. A hiker plods uphill toward us.

"*Ça, c'est dur*—this is hard," he says, wiping sweat from his eyes.

"*Oui, c'est dur,*" one of our party agrees, "*Mais pas trop mal*—but not too bad."

1990

SEARCHING FOR SIMBA

I FLY south at dawn above the basin of the Nile. I follow a track from Cairo and Khartoum to Kenya's Great Rift Valley, a 40-mile-wide trough of grass and scrub. The dull gray glint of the valley floor soon gives way to a luminous wash of copper tan.

Every fold and hummock is picked out in shadow. Sunrise fills the sky. The empty and austere African veldt pales to the color of a lion's skin.

*

I have come to Kenya to take part in one of the last great travel adventures: a journey across an upland plain in search of lion, elephant and antelope, with nights under canvas in unfenced wilderness camps protected from game by perimeter fires and spear-carrying watchmen.

There are 10 in our party. Our guide is a tough young outdoorsman named Simon Zola. At an introductory briefing at a Nairobi hotel—safaris begin and end in the Kenyan capital—he covers the essentials:

Winter Passage

"Don't take pictures of people without their permission. Don't walk barefoot. Don't under any circumstances wander away from camp unescorted."

He describes the amenities: a staff of 12 to look after us; spacious walk-in tents, each with a shaded veranda at one end and a discreetly partitioned latrine and bucket shower at the other.

"The toilet is a hole in the ground with a seat over it," he says matter-of-factly. "We call it a long drop."

There is a hint of a smile, nothing more. I like him instantly.

*

From Nairobi, our road south furrows the flat, grassy heartland of equatorial East Africa. We travel in a convoy of three four-wheel-drive Toyota Land Cruisers.

There are no more than four passengers to a vehicle. The drivers, all with long experience in rough terrain, double as mechanics and game spotters. Simon rides in the lead.

At Namanga, on Kenya's border with Tanzania, under the loom of Mt. Kilimanjaro, we strike off east to the western edge of a gritty and gullied game reserve, Amboseli National Park. The staff has preceded us and set up camp in a wood of umbrella acacias.

There are olive-green tents with zip flaps. They contain night tables, comfortable cots, director's chairs. Close by are a dining tent and a kitchen tent. From a propane burner and wood-fired iron box, Toto, the cook, will produce daily miracles: delicious soups, savory roasts, masterful puddings and pies.

Searching for Simba

*

At 5:30 in the morning, it is still dark. Outside my tent a pressure lamp has been lit and a wash basin filled with hot water.

The air is cool. The dawn is an ashen smudge as we set off in the Land Cruisers, ceiling hatches open for game viewing. Soon the day brightens. Kilimanjaro rises clear and massive in the early light. Its frozen cap gleams.

We scatter shoals of zebra and wildebeest. Giraffe amble across our path with their queer hobby-horse gait.

We see a cheetah tear at the belly of a fresh kill, a once-graceful gazelle fawn. On the limb of a dead tree, two vultures hunch their dark shoulders. They wait, patiently, for the cheetah to feed and depart.

We push through juniper scrub and high elephant grass. We see glossy ibises and white-headed fish eagles. A huge bull elephant kicks a ponderous forefoot at tussocks of grass, loosening the soil.

We have become spectators in a diorama of prehistory. For hours, enthralled, we stand in the hatches of our vehicles and look out upon the unfolding tableau of morning on an African plain.

*

Seroni, like all the camp watchmen, is a Maasai warrior, or *moran*. He belongs to a tribe with a legendary reputation for physical courage. He is tall and slender. The lobes of his ears have been stretched into misshapen loops. He wears garlands of

Winter Passage

beads around his neck and wrists. He wears a cloak of red plaid.

In one hand he carries a broad-bladed spear; in the other, a knobkerrie of carved hardwood. He calls it a *rungu*. I say, "knobkerrie." He laughs, repeating the word very slowly.

In the afternoon, he beckons me to follow him. We leave camp and trek across the plain. We come across the tracks and spoor of animals.

"*Swala*," he says, pointing to a cloven hoofprint. This is the Swahili word for gazelle. "*Tembo*"—elephant. We do not see the splayed pad of *simba,* or lion.

For the first time, I notice the decorative scarring of Seroni's shoulder, a ladder of glazed skin. We round his mud-hut village, but do not enter, then retrace our steps to camp.

*

Our group shakes down into safari routine. Days invariably begin with a long game drive, followed by breakfast, lunch and a siesta in camp. Then out again for a second, longer, ramble in the bush.

As light drains from the sky, we return for hot showers and for drinks in front of a roaring log blaze.

Supper is around eight. The dining tent, lit by candles and pressure lamps, shimmers with crystal and starched napery. Over mushroom soup or gooseberry pie, we listen to the coughs and chuffs of nearby wildlife.

A zebra barks. A hyena screams. Wind sweeps across the plain, carrying with it the pungent odor of dung and hot dust.

Searching for Simba

*

With our camp gear following by truck, we cross the Mau Escarpment and Loita Plain to a 600-square-mile grassland steppe, the Maasai Mara, one of Africa's richest repositories of wild animals.

Tents are pitched in an olive grove on the west bank of the Mara River, running brown with silt. It is February—height of the dry season—but the rains have come early. The track out of camp has washed away. Seeking game, our vehicles now splash overland through a morass of mud and grass.

The first flush of dawn shows a clearing sky. Dew glitters on the tips of grass stalks, bent by the wind. We climb a ridge to firmer ground and the great plain opens in front of us, gold and green, silver and straw. It stretches from a blunt escarpment in the west to a scribble of blue hills in the east.

I am awed by these immense distances. The only sounds are those of the wind and birdsong. The high plateau is fragrant with the scent of herbs and grasses. The plain swarms with zebra, antelope and buffalo. At our approach, a gazelle leaps stiff-legged with fright. Crowned plovers dive on a jackal that has strayed too close to their nest.

Late in the day, the wind strengthens. In the east the sky is electric blue. It is a menacing sky. In this vast wilderness, we feel small and vulnerable. But Simon has promised us lion, and we push south to the river.

On a bluff above the Mara, we spot our quarry. A big, ma-

Winter Passage

ture lion with a full dark mane lies sleeping under a bit of scrub. A smooth-muscled female sprawls a few yards away. Sated with their morning meal, both beasts breathe rapidly, flanks heaving.

The female catches our scent. She rises onto her forelegs. A second female—half hidden in the grass—is up with four cubs.

The male now blinks, yawns, bares fangs like scimitars. He plays to the gallery. He rubs a yellow eye with his right forefoot. He licks his paw. Then lifting his massive bulk, he ambles off to join the pride.

The sky in the east turns blue-black. Rain gusts in sheets across the plain. Simon shouts to the drivers in Swahili:

"*Twende!*"—"Let's go." The drivers start their engines and we run for camp.

1992

BIG MARY'S HOUSE

BY all accounts, he was a big man. His name was Manus Ferry. He worked as a weaver. He was famous the length of Ireland for cloth of great beauty and strength.

He lived, unmarried, in a whitewashed cottage in the country's remote northwest, in County Donegal; in a hamlet that maps once identified as Dun Luiche, but today is called Dunlewy.

Manus's home was his mother's before him, Big Mary's house. And in the Gaelic-speaking precincts—the Gaeltacht—where the cottage stands, Manus Ferry was known by his mother's name, as Manus Maire Mhor, or Manus Big Mary.

Ireland was like that in the old weaver's day. Now it has changed. Yet to travel in Donegal is to venture into a region where pockets of a Celtic tongue survive and where remnants of an ancient culture can still be found.

*

Manus Ferry's Ireland is hardly the Emerald Isle of song and

Winter Passage

tourist brochure. Depopulated by famine and flight, it is, for the most part, a wilderness of peat bog, crag, and somber moor.

It is also a revelation of landscape. Rain drenches the heath; the rain clears as suddenly as it begins; there is a glitter of sun on grass bent flat by the wind.

The light on the moor deepens to russet and shimmering jade shot through with gold. And along a coast of vivid green, headlands sculpted into fantastic shapes fall sheer to gleaming beaches and a cold blue northern sea.

*

Big Mary's house is now the centerpiece of a folk museum run as a village cooperative by the people of Dunlewy. It lies in the west of Donegal, in an isolated setting on the shores of Lough Dunlewy.

The museum is called Ionad Cois Locha: Lakeside Center. Seamus Gallagher, the villager who manages it, conducts daily tours of the weaver's cottage and a scattering of sheds displaying crude farm implements and other relics of an impoverished past.

As you pass through the rooms where Manus Ferry lived and worked, the man himself becomes a presence felt. Here you see his loom and shuttles of hewn oak, his blackened hearth kettle, his cut-peat ready for the fire.

Here also are his oil lamp and washstand, his plain iron bedstead, his crucifix on one wall. His cotton shirts with yellowing collars hang from a wardrobe door.

Manus Ferry died in 1976. He was 84 years old. Gallagher,

Big Mary's House

who knew him well, recalls a tall man in homespun; a man wary of children.

"I asked him once to learn me to weave," Gallagher tells visitors, using an idiom rooted in Gaelic speech. "He wouldn't say yes, he wouldn't say no. But he never did learn me."

*

Distances in Donegal are deceptively short. West to east, a scant 60 miles separates the boulder-strewn Atlantic coast from the bleak peninsula of Inishowen. And it is about as far again from Inishowen south to the hard-packed sands of Donegal Bay.

But pushing inland from the sea are two vast mountain ranges, the Derryveagh and Bluestack. Roads winding round these natural barriers add interminable miles to any journey.

Manus Ferry sold his cloth at town and village fairs throughout Donegal. From his home on the western flank of the Derryveagh, the route he traveled is one that visitors can easily follow in three- or four-days' driving.

It strikes north on narrow lanes, climbing high above the sea to a pastoral speckled with sheep and brightened by golden furze. At the Gaeltacht village of Gortahork, it veers east through Falcarragh and Dunfanaghy to the sandy coves of Sheephaven Bay.

Beyond Creeslough, the road dips south to the geographic center of the county at Letterkenny. From this old cathedral town, the road winds west over the moors to Glenties, the austere little village that Brian Friel, Ireland's greatest living playwright, immortalized as "Ballybeg." It touches also at Ardara, a

Winter Passage

straggle of white and pastel row houses on Loughros More Bay.

*

Much of the cloth sold in Donegal is woven on Ardara cottage handlooms. And it was here that I met Willie McNelis, one of the village's master craftsmen. He produced goods for commercial buyers for 35 years, but now weaves for his own shop—W. McNelis & Sons—on Front Street, off Main. His shelves bear bolts of homespun, in blues, browns and grays, all with the distinctive white flecking of the best of Donegal tweed.

A weaver from the age of 14, McNelis, in his 80s, is a friendly man with white hair, bright blue eyes, a ruddy face. And like Seamus Gallagher of Dunlewy, he is also a keeper of Ireland's collective folk memory. He, too, recalls Manus Ferry.

"A big man, he was. All the Ferrys were big. His mother was Big Mary, and Manus could not be small, could he?"

*

I drive through the starry night, west from Dunfanaghy. There is a sheen on the sea and the hills are black against the luminous sky.

On the outskirts of Gortahork, I stop at a pub. The place is called Teach Ruori, Rory's House. It is a fine old country pub, low beamed, antler adorned. The air is dense with smoke and noise.

As always on this particular night of the week, a space has been cleared at one end of the bar. Five musicians sit in a semicircle. Their instruments are a flute-like tin whistle, a violin,

Big Mary's House

a mandolin, an accordion, and a goatskin-covered open drum, called a bodhran.

With furious intensity, the musicians play hornpipes, jigs and reels. Patrons drink one another's health, raising glasses of lager and stout. As the music rattles and skirls, the drinkers yelp and stamp their feet.

The bodhran player is a girl with a sallow face, dark hair. At the end of a set, she lowers her head to the drum's wooden frame. One hand damps the back of the instrument; with the other, she strikes a slow, muffled beat.

"This is a song about the return of Paddy," the bodhran player says. "About Paddy's return from wandering in America."

The drinkers fall silent. The familiar lament, in a minor key, touches the strain of melancholy that lies close to the surface of Irish life. In a clear, sweet, high voice, the bodhran player sings:

"Welcome poor Paddy home...."

2017

TWICE AN IMMIGRANT

THE people in the image form a tableau. Two boys, brothers, stand stiffly. Their mother, a handsome woman in her thirties, bends slightly forward. The only animated figure is that of the child, a pretty little girl of two. She is daughter of the woman, sister of the boys. Oblivious of her surroundings, she prances about. She has no way of knowing she has boarded a wartime British troopship—life rafts lashed to the deck—and will shortly embark from an Egyptian seaport on the first leg of a longer journey whose safe completion is uncertain. Twenty-one years later, the girl in the photo and I will marry.

This is an immigrant's story. It is a story of dislocation and of renewal, and it begins many years ago, in the early days of the Second World War. Caroline Littell, who in later life would make her home in western New York, was born in 1939 in Cairo, Egypt, a country then a protectorate of Britain. Her baptismal name in the Catholic Church was Caroline Jane Penelope Byass. Her father, Lt. Col. F.W. Byass, commanded a regiment

Twice an Immigrant

of British armor in the North African desert war against German and Italian forces.

In the summer of 1941, with the Wehrmacht's Panzer divisions threatening Cairo, Caroline and her brothers, Charles, 13, and David, 11, were evacuated by rail to Suez, gateway to the Red Sea and Indian Ocean. Their mother, Constance Mary, accompanied them as far as the port. She would remain in Egypt as a naval cypher clerk. A pair of elderly nannies seeking passage home to England—the Misses Weston and Backhouse—had care of the children.

Suez in those days was a busy place, with once-great passenger liners requisitioned as troopships disgorging their cargoes of men and weaponry and embarking displaced colonials and prisoners of war for the long, slow voyages to South Africa and Britain. The two nannies and their charges boarded *RMS (Royal Mail Ship) Empress of Russia*, a three-funnel coal burner built in Scotland in 1913 for the Canadian Pacific Line's Far East service. The vessel was bound for Durban, on the east coast of South Africa.

From England, my brother-in-law David Byass writes:

"From Suez to Durban there were on board about 200 Italian prisoners who were allowed on deck for one hour a day, otherwise locked below. At Durban we were dumped ashore so that *Empress of Russia* could go back to Suez for another load."

After a week in a hotel, the children and their nannies traveled overland to Cape Town, in the country's west. There they

Winter Passage

joined another transport, *RMS Franconia*, a single-funnel Cunard liner dating from 1923. She was a big ship but a slow ship. Her twin-screw propulsion could push her along at not much more than 16 knots, or 18 miles an hour. It was a rate of speed barely adequate to outrun the German submarines known to be operating in African waters.

Franconia's master, James Bisset, takes up the story. "[We] loaded a cargo of foodstuffs at Durban and at Cape Town," he would recall. "On 20th July 1941 [we] left Cape Town, alone, with a cargo of 3070 tons and 300 passengers, homeward bound for Liverpool. I was directed to proceed…across the South Atlantic to Trinidad Island, at the south-eastern edge of the Caribbean Sea. That region was under the protection of the United States Navy."

Bisset was a bluff, burly seaman noted for the part he had played, as a young ship's officer, in the 1912 rescue of *Titanic* survivors. His long career in sail and steam would be capped by appointment to war commands of the world's two most famous liners, *Queen Mary* and *Queen Elizabeth*, hauling hundreds of thousands of American troops across the North Atlantic.

Now, at 58, and with the safety of *Franconia*'s passengers his chief concern, Bisset had shaped a course "less liable to U-boat attack than on the route along the west coast of Africa and across the Bay of Biscay." As an added precaution, he had ordered lifeboats freed from their cradles and "swung out over the side, ready for immediate lowering."

Twice an Immigrant

In the summer of 1941, with German Panzer divisions threatening Cairo, a two-year-old war evacuee from Egypt, Caroline Byass, prances on deck of a steamer that will carry her and her two brothers on the first leg of a journey to safety in England.

In his 1961 memoir, "Commodore," Bisset provides a laconic account of his ship's unescorted flight from danger. "*Franconia*," he writes, "made the passage from Cape Town to Trinidad, 5628 miles, in fifteen days, at an average speed of 15 knots [17 miles an hour], and anchored at Port of Spain on 4th August.

"After taking on 2300 tons of oil and 943 tons of fresh water, we put to sea on 5th August. Twelve days later, we let go the anchor in the Mersey. The passage from Trinidad…was 4499 miles by zigzag."

From Suez to Liverpool, the Byass children had covered some 15,000 miles in eight weeks. But of the many memories the brothers had of their adventure, one, they've told me, especially

Winter Passage

stood out. They recalled stationing themselves at opposite sides of *Franconia's* deck and of careening Caroline between them in her pram, catching the child on the vessel's downward roll and sending her back on the upward swing. Their baby sister, they reported, loved every minute of it. Nannies Weston and Backhouse were not amused.

Caroline spent the rest of the war with a grandmother in a suburb of London; her brothers attended their father's old boarding school, Wellington, 40 miles west of the capital. Several months after the children had sailed from Suez, Lt. Col. Byass was killed in action in the Egyptian desert.

I've headed this reminiscence "Twice an Immigrant." For there would be a second journey to a new life in a strange and unfamiliar country. It came a couple of decades later, when Caroline booked passage on *SS France*, one of the fastest and most beautiful luxury liners of the big-ship era.

Launched in 1960, she was an enormous vessel, more than 1,000 feet long, with 12 decks and a distinguishing pair of raked, winged funnels. Her powerful turbines and quadruple screws could produce a cruising speed of 30 knots, or 35 miles an hour. The new ship, sailing under the house flag of the French Line, entered transatlantic service—Le Havre-Southampton (England)-New York—in February 1962.

In early March of the liner's inaugural year, the 22-year-old Caroline Byass boarded at Southampton. The crossing to New York took five days. On arrival, the young immigrant walked

Twice an Immigrant

down a canopied gangway and through a dark, dank pier shed to West Street, in lower Manhattan. A porter followed with her single piece of hold baggage, an oversized footlocker, and Caroline stepped out into the United States.

The story ends with an epilogue: Although she and I had met and lived in Paris, we married in New York. We moved a few years later, with two sons, to a university town in a rural hinterland of our state. Caroline became an American citizen; she achieved distinction as a professional photographer of great flair and artistry; she died in Pasadena, California, on March 18, 2015.

I possess still my wife's footlocker. It is, for me, an amulet of sorts. Its brass latches and corner fittings, once bright, are dulled by the span of more than half a century. A faded steamship label affixed to the lid bears the name of the great French liner she had traveled on. And one can yet make out, in Caroline's unmistakable hand, the accompanying words—New York—that signaled not only her destination, but, I think, what she took to be the broader meaning of that port of entry: less the immigrant's break with a European past but rather an embrace of the new: the freedom of being young in a novel and unfettered society.

ABOUT THE AUTHOR

Alan Littell has worked as a merchant mariner and as a newspaper reporter and editor in Boston and Paris. Best known as a nationally distributed travel journalist—his credits include The New York Times, The Los Angeles Times, The Chicago Tribune and Travel & Leisure Magazine—he is author of a novel of the sea, "Courage," published in 2007 by St. Martin's Press. He is an occasional columnist for three regional newspapers in Western New York, and he lives in Alfred, New York.

www.ingramcontent.com/pod-product-compliance
Lightning Source LLC
Chambersburg PA
CBHW061439040426
42450CB00007B/1128